HOW TO
CHANGE
YOUR MIND

HOW TO CHANGE YOUR MIND

USING MODERN PSYCHOLOGICAL METHODS AND THE WISDOM OF EDGAR CAYCE

by Peter Alimaras, Ph.D.

A.R.E. Press • Virginia Beach • Virginia

A.R.E. Press
Sixty-Eighth & Atlantic Avenue
P.O. Box 656
Virginia Beach, VA 23451-0656

Library of Congress Cataloging-in-Publication Data
Alimaras, Peter, 1940-
How to change your mind : using modern psychological
methods and the wisdom of Edgar Cayce / by Peter Alimaras.
p.   cm.
Includes bibliographical references.
ISBN 0-87604-371-6 (trade paper)
1. Parapsychology. 2. Adjustment (Psychology). 3. Self-help
techniques. 4. Cayce, Edgar, 1877-1945. Edgar Cayce readings.
I. Title
BF1045.A34A46   1997
131-dc21   96-46154

Cover design by Kim Cohen

Contents

Preface

*As a psychologist, I have always been intrigued by the te-*nacity of the human personality. By the time we become adults, we show characteristic ways of thinking, feeling, and behaving. These appear to be automatic patterns that are repeated over and over. To use an old cliche, we are "creatures of habit." Psychological disorders also reflect habit patterns, but these are maladaptive, or bad ones. While people who suffer from such problems will readily acknowledge the idea of being "stuck" in their dilemmas, others find the notion of habit offensive, as it portrays something that operates on its own. Habit takes away the feeling of control in life or the idea that we have free will.

At a fundamental level, free will does exist, and we can effect changes in our lives. Yet, on an everyday basis, this is more illusory than it seems, for we react more than we act. To appreciate this, take a quick inventory of the way your body works. Here you can see the operation of a marvelous piece of machinery, from the beating of its heart to the manner in which it fights off disease. You probably have no difficulty acknowledging the mechanics underlying your biological processes. The sense of decision and control is usually assigned to the workings of your mind and to the actions that you take. After all, you decide what you want to think about, how to feel, and how to act. However, these processes, too, may be more automatic than you imagine. Reflect, for a moment, on your personality. Where does your mind take you? Do you drift off to concerns of family, career, or school? Or, maybe you ruminate about a relationship, finances, or your health. Think about how you walk, talk, tie your shoes, eat your food, dance, play softball, and drive your car. Think of what makes you happy, sad, frightened, and angry. Think of your likes and dislikes in life. Isn't it true that these are stable patterns, that they don't change very much?

If this is really the case, it may not matter so much to someone who is happy in life. It becomes a primary concern, however, to the individual suffering from a psychological disorder. Such a person wants desperately to change. How is this done, how can one change? If free will exists at a basic level, yet is not really accessed that much, how can the habitual pattern of the psychological problem be altered?

To answer this question, I ask you to consider the insights derived from one of the most remarkable psychics witnessed by the twentieth century, Edgar Cayce. In a state of complete dissociation, he was able to tap into an unknown source of knowledge and relate information to all sorts of people, for all kinds of problems. These readings, as they became known, provide a coherent view of human nature within the context of esoteric tradition. Included here is a wealth of information about the sources and treatments of psychological disorders. Origins are seen as multifaceted, reflecting the expressions of a soul through a multidimensional journey. Treatments are holistic and aim to harmonize conflicting patterns of spirit, mind, and body. Psychospiritual advice revolves around setting spiritual ideals as foundations for the formation of constructive habit patterns. These are to serve as replacements for those that are psychologically destructive. Establishing such patterns not only results in symptom relief, but in the eventual transformation of personality as a higher essence in life is actualized. Moreover, even though one type of habit is replaced with another, working with spiritual ideals results in a paradoxical increase in personal freedom.

The world view expressed in the readings of Edgar Cayce embraces many areas of knowledge, including, of course, theories in modern psychology. This is especially true regarding its affinity to behavioral psychology, where here, too, psychological disorders are viewed within a framework of maladaptive habit patterns. In this book, I have attempted to reconcile the self-help techniques derived from behavioral psychology and other models with the psychospiritual recommendations of the readings. This will enable you to contemporize the readings, as well as make use of some of the latest strategies available in the treatment of psychological dilemmas.

I invite you now to join me in a most interesting adventure. Psychological disorders, while seemingly rigid, are by no means permanent. They can be viewed as opportunities for growth, both on a personal level and, more important, on a spiritual level. You can work with your problem, rather than against it and, as a result, attain benefits beyond your expectations. You can change your mind.

I wish to thank my dear wife Linda and my wonderful children Steven and Anastasia for their patience and encouragement in the preparation of this book. I should also like to express my gratitude to three other special people in my life, my mother Tessie, my brother Nick, and my cousin Helen, whose lives serve as inspirations for anyone wishing to work with the readings. A special thanks also goes to my editors at A.R.E. for their assistance and help.

PART 1

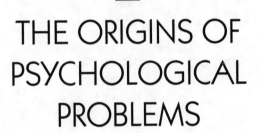

THE ORIGINS OF PSYCHOLOGICAL PROBLEMS

1

Problems, Problems, Problems!

... to each individual ... let it be stressed that the attitude of self ... is to be ... a constructive thing throughout; and we will find this can be made to grow, and the problems become ... opportunities rather than stumbling stones ...

Edgar Cayce reading 641-6[1]

"I can't cope!" "I can't go on like this any more!" "I'm not happy!" "Why can't these problems go away?" How many times have we felt like this and looked for answers to our dilemmas? Psychological disorders are common events in the lives of many people. They can occur at any time, and in many instances seem to make up a central part of personality for as long as one remembers. Sometimes they seem to get better or to go away completely. More often they appear to become permanent fixtures. They cause considerable distress in the way we feel and affect the way we think. They also incapacitate us at work and school, and interfere with our abilities to relate to oth-

ers. In short, they can make life pretty miserable.

Psychological problems come in a variety of sizes and shapes as the following examples show:

Catherine is always on edge and worried about something. On one day she's anxious about possible misfortune befalling her children and on another about potential financial problems. She even becomes apprehensive about making an appointment on time. Catherine lives in a "what if" world and always catastrophizes about something. She seems unable to control her worries and feels badly since they interfere with her desire to enjoy her family and friends. They also make her quite irritable and interfere with her sleep. Catherine has an emotional problem referred to as generalized anxiety disorder.

Mark has a tremendous fear of flying. Even the sight of an airport makes him nervous. Every time he visits his brother he takes a two-day trip by railroad rather than a short airplane flight. Mark's problem has recently affected his job as his new promotion requires that he travel out of town. He doesn't know if he can handle this. Mark's disorder is called a specific phobia, situational type.

John suffers from a panic disorder with agoraphobia. This means that he has unexpected panic attacks in situations which are not at all threatening to him. What is it like to have a panic attack? Try to remember if you were ever in a very dangerous situation which caused you to panic. You might have felt like you were about to explode or bust, that you were losing your grip on reality, that you were going crazy. You might have also experienced dizziness, palpitations, sweating, or other reactions. John has these very same feelings in nonthreatening situations, and he can't understand why. Because he is always worried about getting these attacks, he tends to stay home much of the time. If he has to go out, he does so with a great deal of anxiety.

Jennifer has an obsessive-compulsive disorder. Her problem involves persistent thoughts that she will be contaminated by harmful germs which she imagines to be present everywhere. To avoid such contamination, she is very careful in the way she touches things. Even shaking hands with someone becomes a problem for her. To deal with these obsessions, Jennifer spends a great deal of time cleaning, and this seems to dominate her life. Although Jennifer sees her thoughts as unreasonable and tries to suppress them, she cannot.

Marie has been feeling depressed and "down in the dumps" for the past few weeks. She constantly talks about how wonderful life is for other people and how unfortunate she is. She sees herself as worthless, as a loser. She shows no interest in activities that were once enjoyed, saying that she doesn't care about these things anymore. Lately she's been having difficulty falling asleep at night, even though she feels tired all the time. In addition, she's eating more than usual and gaining weight. At times she feels that she'd be better off dead. Marie is suffering from a major depressive disorder.

George is distressed because he drinks too much. He says that he always tries to cut down, but cannot. In addition, he sees that he needs more and more alcohol to experience the effect that he likes. Recently George went for a medical exam and was told that he'd better cut out his drinking as it was affecting his heart. Despite this warning, he can't seem to stop. George has alcohol dependence.

These problems and many others show the kinds of suffering involved in psychological disorders. As you see, they can cause considerable emotional distress as well as impair one's ability to function, whether at school, on the job, within the family, in interpersonal situations, and in many other areas of life. Perhaps you or someone you know can identity with these kinds of problems. If so, you'd probably like to know what causes them, as well as how to deal with them. These are not easy questions to answer. In fact, there are no definitive answers. If you were to look at what the experts say, you'd see a number of different theories, each making different philosophical and psychological assumptions about personality, both normal and abnormal. To make things more confusing, these theories often clash with each other around key issues such as the effects of heredity and environment, the importance of childhood, the role of unconscious dynamics, and other key issues.

Let's take Marie's depression as an example. Suppose she decides to get professional help for her problem and visits a psychoanalyst. This type of therapist would assume that her depression was the result of an unconscious conflict originating during her childhood years, involving early feelings of sexuality and aggression. His treatment recommendation would be a long-term, in-depth approach enabling Marie to gain insight into the source of her depression and become symptom free.

Marie decides to go for a second opinion and contacts a humanistic psychologist. While he also informs her that she needs insight therapy, he indicates that her depression stems from her inability to express her real self. He relates this to her upbringing, where her parents attempted to shape her personality. Although they thought this was in her best interests, they effected an incongruence in her personality between her natural tendencies and their wishes. It was this incongruence which related to her depression.

At this point, Marie is confused with the conflicting information she has received and goes to another professional, this time an existential psychotherapist. Here she learns that her depression relates to a basic sense of loneliness that all people share due to their inability to fathom the meaning of their existence. Again, a long-term therapy is recommended through which she would learn to find purpose in life and cope with her existential dilemmas.

More confused at this point, she goes to another professional, this time a behavioral psychologist. He concludes that her depression relates to a lack of rewarding experiences in her interpersonal life due to her inadequate social skills. No mention is made of unconscious conflicts, incongruences, or existential crises. He recommends a short-term group therapy approach where Marie can learn positive ways of interacting with others and in time develop rewarding relationships.

At this point, Marie doesn't know what to do. She listens to a friend who suggests one final consultation with a psychiatrist. The psychiatrist is quick to dispute all other therapeutic approaches and offers instead a biochemical interpretation for her depression. He traces it to a malfunction in the neurotransmission process of her nervous system and offers her relief with the drug prozac (fluoxetine).

Totally perplexed by the different interpretations and recommendations she received, Marie decides to do some reading on her own. She looks at the research studies on the effects of psychotherapy with the hope of determining the best course of action for her depression. Unfortunately, what she discovers doesn't help her very much. She learns that no one therapy works better than another and that sometimes people get better by themselves. She also learns that a very important factor that helps the healing process relates to the expectations a person has about it. This is called the placebo effect and, as we'll discuss later on, plays a major role in all healing.

As you can see it's not that easy to attack an emotional problem. It's not like having the flu. With a flu, you can go to your doctor and get some pretty specific treatment recommendations. If you were to go for a second opinion, chances are good that you'd be given the same kind of advice. The same is not true for psychological problems. The reason for this is that this area is still in its infancy. While there are many theories out there, there is little consensus among them. This, in turn is due to the difficulty of the subject area itself, as well as to the limitations of the current methodology. Experts in the mental health field are, after all, only people trying to understand other people. They use the best research methods available and attempt to be as objective as possible in their efforts. The present century has indeed witnessed some extraordinary conclusions reached by many who devoted their lives in this direction. Who has not heard the names of Freud, Jung, Rogers, or Skinner? Hopefully, in the years to come, all present theoretical perspectives will be incorporated into one unified theory of the abnormal personality.

2

How Did I Get This Way?
The View of Edgar Cayce

But when an entity, a soul, uses a period of manifestation—
in whatever realm of consciousness—to its *own indulgencies,*
then there is need for the lesson, or for the soul understanding or interpreting, or to become aware of the error of its way.
Edgar Cayce reading 815-7

Do not look on personalities. Look on the individuality of the
individual, and know that comes from the spiritual and not
from the personal self. This will make it much easier for
decisions to be made in relationship with things, circumstances and individuals.   Edgar Cayce reading 2582-3

Who is Edgar Cayce, and what role does he play in the
attempt to understand psychological disorders? Most
people probably have never heard of him, yet he was one
of the most fascinating personalities of our time. Born
and raised in Kentucky in the latter part of the nine-
teenth century, he displayed in his life a remarkable
manifestation of paranormal ability. As related in Tom
Sugrue's biographical account, *There Is a River,*[1] Edgar
Cayce appeared to have several unusual experiences in
his youth which culminated in an uncanny ability to diagnose and treat all kinds of human problems. As a child,
he claimed to have imaginary friends. What was unusual

7

about this was his ability to perceive them and to interact with them. When he was thirteen, he experienced an apparition of an angelic figure who promised to fulfill his innermost desires. What the young Cayce requested was the ability to help other people. Soon after he spontaneously developed the ability to absorb into memory any material placed near him while he slept. This enabled him to excel in his school performance which, up to that time, had been quite poor. When he was fifteen, he was hurt while playing a ball game. After behaving irrationally for several hours, he quieted down and somehow suggested a successful treatment for his own injury. Each of these events can obviously be explained within the purview of ordinary experiences by appealing to such factors as overactive imagination, photographic memory, coincidence, spontaneous remission, and the like. However, when looked at within the context of the full Cayce phenomenon, they may well be interpreted in an altogether different light.

The year was 1901, and Edgar Cayce was twenty-three years old. He developed some sort of ailment which included an inability to speak above a whisper. When this failed to clear up after a reasonable period of time, he was diagnosed with aphonia. Aphonia is a type of psychological problem known as conversion disorder. It is assumed to be brought on by conflict and stress. One of the treatment approaches, both today and in Cayce's time, is hypnosis. This was attempted but proved unsuccessful. A year passed with Cayce resigned to his destiny. He even embarked upon a career in photography at this time, feeling that this required minimal use of his voice. Then a New York doctor recommended that hypnosis be attempted once again but in a different way. He said that once under hypnosis, Cayce should be asked to talk about his condition, to indicate what the problem was and what could be done about it. The rationale for this approach related to various earlier accounts of apparent psychic abilities occurring under hypnosis. With the help of an acquaintance, Al Layne, Cayce agreed to try this. What followed was simply amazing. The date was March 31, 1901. Cayce put himself in a trance state, and Layne asked him to indicate what was wrong with his throat. Soon Cayce began speaking in a normal manner and described a partial paralysis of his vocal cord muscles caused by psychological factors. He said that the problem could be helped by hypnotic suggestion given to increase the circulation in this area, and Layne proceeded to do this. About twenty minutes later, the sleeping Cayce said that the condition had cleared up. He requested another suggestion to restore his circulation to normal and to awaken him. Following this, he woke up with the full use of his voice. What was a tenacious condition had apparently been healed by a most unorthodox treatment.

While Cayce was understandably happy at this turn of events, he found it to be the beginning of another, more perplexing dilemma. For it soon became apparent that in his self-hypnotic state, he could diagnose and treat other people for a variety of medical conditions just as easily as he treated himself for his aphonia. Moreover, the individual making the request didn't even have to be physically present to receive this help. The information from his trance-like state became known as a "reading" and was to present Cayce with a major psychological conflict for many years.

Cayce was a simple man with a limited education. He was also a very religious man. His life's goals revolved around the traditions of his day within the context of Christian tenets: marriage, family, and career. All of these clashed with the paranormal abilities evident in his psychic readings. He questioned not only what he was doing, but how he was able to do it. What especially bothered him was the reason for his ability. He constantly looked for purpose and meaning in it. He was both uncomfortable and frightened with the readings and yet felt that perhaps they related to his true goal in life. He constantly thought about his earlier vision of the angelic figure and his expressed desire to help people. He wanted a rationale for the readings, especially within a religious sense. Were they a gift from God or a curse from the devil?

Cayce met numerous people who expressed interest in his work. Their reasons ranged from materialistic gains to philosophical concerns. People talked to him and talked about him. Some wanted to associate with him, while others wanted nothing to do with him. He was evaluated by numerous physicians, themselves seeking answers to the enigma he presented. He was written up in many newspaper articles. In short, Edgar Cayce managed to achieve a most undesired notoriety. The bottom line was that, although Cayce gave readings for people who asked, he was conflicted about them and attempted to maintain a normal lifestyle. It wasn't until more than twenty years after he treated himself for aphonia that he made a decision regarding the importance of the readings. It was at this time that he converted his photography studio into an office and hired a stenographer to record the readings.

It was also around this time that he met Arthur Lammers, a man who was to introduce another major change in Cayce's life. Lammers had a deep interest in philosophy, astrology, and the paranormal and asked Cayce for information related to these while in trance. What followed were ideas and concepts that were totally incongruent with Cayce's belief system, especially with regard to his religious tenets. Most troublesome was the concept of reincarnation, the idea that humans are born again and again into successive lives. It took a while for

Cayce to accept this notion and to assimilate it into his Christian orientation. Thereafter, Cayce began giving two kinds of readings. In addition to what had become known as "physical readings," where medical advice was offered, he also gave "life readings." The life reading was more of a psychological evaluation describing an individual's personality conflicts within the context of relevant previous-life experiences. Both types of readings offered constructive recommendations for positive changes. Cayce also gave readings on general topics to people requesting these. From all these readings, many interesting ideas presented themselves. In addition to medicine, they dealt with issues in such areas as religion, philosophy, history, archaeology, and psychic phenomena.

Before we examine how these readings look at psychological problems, let's pause for a moment to see what you're thinking so far. Does the Cayce story make any sense to you? Based on this brief overview, it may be difficult to answer such a question. Suppose, however, that as you read more about Edgar Cayce, you became convinced of the validity of the man, his life, his conflicts, and especially his paranormal abilities. Could you then answer this question? It still might present a problem for you, as it goes against common sense. After all, we know that knowledge is acquired through experience. How can a man with a limited education go into a hypnotic state and appear to tap an unlimited source of information? Yet this is exactly what he did. So what do we do with him? Unless we want to tuck him away someplace or consider him as some freak of nature, it behooves us to look at him very carefully and to perhaps reexamine our common-sense view of the world, especially as it pertains to the way we understand ourselves. So I ask you to put aside for a while your everyday notions of how the world works and see what the readings have to say about psychological disorders. Then decide for yourself.

On the one hand, by providing a theoretical framework for emotional problems, the readings only add to the ambiguity present in contemporary psychology. Yet, they have a different appeal, as they make no claims to success. They only suggest that you try them out for yourself and see if they work. They stress application, or doing something. The attitude in working with the readings is like that of a scientist. The scientist develops a hypothesis from various sources and tests its value by engaging in some sort of research. The outcome provides feedback on the validity of the hypothesis. In the same manner, the readings offer many recommendations for handling psychological problems which can be tested whether one is looking for symptom relief or for a more profound transformation of personality. Moreover, in most cases, they advise self-help rather than psychological counseling or other professional intervention.

To understand the Cayce view on psychological disorders, it is first necessary to see how it conceptualizes reality. The readings exemplify what may be called an *esoteric* approach to nature. Such an approach contrasts sharply with the *exoteric* method of the scientist. The exoteric worldview assumes that the basis of reality is physical or material. What it considers as real, and really important, are objects like trees, houses, cars, animals, planets, and so on. These things make up what is referred to as *objective reality*. What about the human mind? In general, this is usually seen in one of two ways. Some believe that it is identical to the functioning of the nervous system, especially the brain. Here, thinking relates to the brain in action. The other premise is that the mind is qualitatively different from the brain but plays a passive, limited role in human nature. Either way, in the exoteric worldview, psychological problems ultimately have physical roots.

In contrast, the esoteric paradigm of the Cayce readings assumes that there's more to reality than meets the eye. It tells us that reality is simultaneously both one and multidimensional in essence. It is one because it is based in one source, and this is God or *spirit*. As unlimited creative energy forever emanating love, spirit is the essence of life itself. It makes up everything, both visible and invisible. It does this by using *mind*. While this word means many things, in the bigger picture of reality mind relates to a process of shaping spiritual energy into patterns or forms. Think of it as something like a pattern-generating device. In the esoteric tradition, patterns differ according to their "vibrations," and these differences define various spiritual dimensions or levels of reality. This notion reflects the multidimensionality of nature. While there are many levels of reality, three basic patterns are the spiritual, the mental, and the physical. The physical world, or objective reality, is then a manifestation of spirit that is molded by mind. The creation of patterns at any level of reality is guided by the action of *free will*. This is a most important aspect of reality as it allows for diversity in the expression of patterns. It also accounts for the individuality of these patterns.

What about the human mind? The readings tell us that it reflects an interaction of spiritual, mental, and physical patterns as they revolve around and are continually being affected by one's will. This interaction results in the characteristic way in which ordinary reality comes across to us, or what is referred to as *subjective reality*. At this state, we all see ourselves as having minds and bodies and existing in a world. At other levels of reality, however, the quality of the mental experience shifts, so that things come across in different ways. While this again reflects an apparent multiplicity in nature, everything emanates from one creative source or spirit, and a oneness or unity permeates all reality. This is a basic premise of the Cayce paradigm.

The readings also highlight the primacy of subjective reality or the human mind. It is in the arena of consciousness that the drama of one's life is played out, and it is here where solutions to problems are found. Psychological disorders are also viewed within this context. They represent mental anguish stemming from conflicts in a system of interacting spiritual, mental, and physical factors. Solutions are found only by working with the mind. More important, it is through mind that one ultimately understands and appreciates basic truths. The reason for this is that ordinary, everyday experiences reflect the bigger picture of reality and, as such, become educative. Another way of saying this is that the *microcosm* is a shadow of the *macrocosm*. By looking at ordinary life, both in its good and bad elements, we can slowly come to see the workings of a marvelous, intelligent, guiding reality.

As an analogy, imagine that spiritual energy consists of H_2O and that the mind forms a radiator. At one point the H_2O becomes steam, and it's contained within the radiator. The radiator then defines the shape that the steam takes. The previously undifferentiated, formless H_2O is now expressed as steam and has a pattern to it. Moreover, as radiators come in different sizes and shapes, the steam can take on different patterns. Will is the director of this. Imagine now that the radiator breaks down and fills up with water. In time, the water turns to ice. Regardless of whether it contains steam, water, or ice, the radiator still defines the shape that is assumed. This may help you to understand the paradox of the oneness and multiplicity in nature. Just as H_2O can appear as vapor, water, or ice, so too can spiritual energy be patterned by mind under the direction of will and appear in different ways in different realities. So what we call our subjective and objective realities ultimately represent one pattern of spiritual energy coming across in two different ways.

Before considering how psychological problems fit into this paradigm, let's first take a common-sense view of personality and begin by looking more at the human mind. If you were to examine your mental experiences, you would probably agree that they come across in different ways at different times. For most of the day, you are in an ordinary state of consciousness and are using your mind in a specific way. When you're asleep, however, you're in another state of consciousness, and your mind is operating in a very different manner. An easy way to see this is to examine the way your mind is working right now as you read this book and to compare it with how it was functioning during last night's dream. Notice how rational you are right now, compared to the bizarre quality of the dream. In addition to dreaming, there are other alterations of consciousness, such as hypnosis, meditation, and drug-induced states.

While personality relates to the totality of your subjective experiences, it is usually considered within the context of ordinary consciousness and the objective reality that goes along with it. If you ask yourself, "What makes up my personality?" or "Who am I?" you would see that the basic "you" consists of both mind and body. Part of the way you define yourself refers to your subjective world, as, for instance, when you say something like "I am intelligent." Another part relates to your objective world, as in "I am tall." Let's look at this more closely.

If you were to examine the kinds of events that make up your ordinary conscious experiences, or the things that go on in your mind during the day, you would notice many different processes. What is called the sensory/perceptual component refers to how you apprehend and interpret the world around you. When you see a beautiful sunset, smell a rose, or hear a song on the radio, you are utilizing this process. You also have ideas about things or you think in certain ways. This is the cognitive component of consciousness that can be seen in such processes as ruminating over the day's events, solving problems in your head, and daydreaming. In addition there are the various desires and drives you have, which make up the motivational aspect of consciousness. You also have feelings, which reflect the emotional component of mental life. These include states like happiness, sadness, fear, anger, and others. Finally, there is something called intuition. Intuition incorporates all of the other processes but is experienced as coming from an undefinable source. This can be seen when you have a "gut" reaction to something but can't quite put your finger on why.

While the subjective world is a flux of sensory/perceptual, cognitive, motivational, emotional, and intuitive processes, the objective world consists of external objects and events. These include everything you come in contact with, like cars, trees, cats, water, rainstorms, chairs—everything in your environment. A very important part of this environment is, of course, your physical body. We can also look at the body as having components. There is an external part, which represents such things as height, weight, skin color, and so on, and an internal part consisting of cells, tissues, organs, and the like. In addition, we can also refer to what the body does or to its behavior. This refers to such actions as walking, talking, running, blinking, sneezing, and so on.

Let's put this all together now and look at personality as made up of various characteristics or traits. Each trait is a complex structure that reflects components of the mind and body in various ways and by different degrees. When you say, "I am female," or "I am thin," you are referring to an external aspect of your body. If you describe yourself as having high blood pressure, you are talking about the internal, physiological functioning of your body. When you say such things as "I play basketball," or "I'm always in a hurry," you're making reference to your behavior. Trait components that focus on your thoughts, feelings, and other subjective elements would be seen in statements like, "I'm nervous," or "I feel lucky today."

Although personality traits can be analyzed like this along parameters of mind and body, most traits involve both aspects which interact with each other. Consider a man whose life revolves around sports. One of his favorite activities is tennis. How is this expressed? To begin with, he has a desire to play tennis (motivational). He reads a local newspaper to see what courts are available (sensory/perceptual). He feels elated that a nearby court is open (emotional). He thinks about calling up somebody to join him (cognitive). He phones his friend, they go to the court and play (behavioral). He has a hunch he will lose (intuitive). During the game he sprains his ankle and has to stop (physiological).

Psychological problems can also be examined like this. A woman who is depressed says that she feels sad (emotional) and has no desire to do anything (motivational). She cries a great deal (behavioral) and thinks a lot about death (cognitive). She sees things in her life as bleak and views everybody else as happy (sensory/perceptual). She also has a hormonal imbalance (physiological) which may be linked to her condition. She feels that her suffering has some higher meaning and purpose (intuitive).

Trait components interact in a continuous manner, affecting each other and constituting a pattern. This pattern is highly individualistic. Each trait is unique or "tailor made." Think of "generosity," for example. What does this refer to? While two people can be described as generous, each may show this in a very different way. One person can be generous with material things, the other generous with time. Similarly, one individual described as "careless" may be so in keeping appointments, while another may be careless with the use of credit cards. These same kinds of differences also are seen in psychological problems. One individual's "anxiety" may involve unrealistic ruminations about financial disaster while another's may reflect catastrophic thinking about health problems.

Another way of looking at personality traits is in terms of endurance. When something is enduring, it lasts. Some personality traits are more enduring than others. They seem to be with us for a long time, like permanent fixtures in personality. Other characteristics are more ephemeral. They come and go. This includes such things as tastes in clothes, hair styles, interests in music, political beliefs, and so on. Did you ever look at some old pictures of yourself taken years ago? Your tastes in clothing then were probably very different from what they are now, and you would be very uncomfortable dressed that way today. Such characteristics define less enduring personality traits. Psychologically distressing traits can also be examined this way. Sometimes they are long lasting, and at other times short-lived. The depressed woman in the above example might remember feeling sad even as a little girl, or she may say that she was always a happy person and only recently began feeling depressed.

Just as each personality trait represents a unique pattern of interacting processes with differences in endurance, so too does personality as a whole. Personality itself is a pattern of interrelated traits, with each trait influencing the others and in turn being influenced by them. Let's go back to our sports-minded individual. Suppose that, in addition to his interest in sports, he has a high need for achievement. This trait would color his interest in sports, so that winning a game would be very important to him. He would be very competitive and feel a great sense of accomplishment whenever he won. Losing would result in frustration, irritability, and anger. Now what would be the case if he had a low need for achievement? He might engage in sports for fun, attempt to win, but not become upset if he lost, and perhaps he would even allow others to win to make them feel good. Notice how the traits pertaining to sports and achievement affect each other.

The same can be seen with psychological problems. The depressed woman in the above example might interpret her plight as God's punishment and obsess over past sins if she sees herself as a "religious" person. If she was "atheistic," on the other hand, she might instead see her hormonal imbalance as the roots of her depression.

Personality traits are centered around a *self-awareness*. This is a vital aspect of personality, as it defines what being human is all about. Self-awareness is the experience of your existence. Every time you use the words "I" or "me," you are referring to it. Personality traits revolve around this central "I-ness" and are expressions of it. It is self-awareness that gives unity to personality. As we have seen, personality traits partake of both subjective and objective aspects of reality and thus paradoxically present us with a duality to our nature. We acknowledge two parts to our personalities, a mind part and a body part. It is self-awareness that allows us to see ourselves as one person.

In conjunction with this, self-awareness ties in with the notion of free will. Free will means that you can effect action in life. It means that you can choose to do things, that you have control over your life. In some instances, this seems obvious, as when you make a decision over what to wear in the morning. At other times, decision making appears more lengthy and exhausting as, for instance, in deciding whether to get married, to make a financial investment, to undergo surgery, and other such concerns. Sometimes we may even feel that we have no choice at all. A man injured in a terrorist bombing may feel that he was the victim of circumstances. What all this means is that, as we experience our personalities in ordinary consciousness, we see different degrees of freedom available to us.

In other states of consciousness, the situation is quite different. When we are dreaming, for example, there is no self-awareness for the most part. Since we are not aware of ourselves, there are no choices to be made, and the dream follows its own directive. If choice were available during dreaming, why would we have nightmares? The exception to this is the lucid dream. Here, one is aware of being in a dream state and can thereby exercise control over its outcome.

Although free will appears to be accessible during ordinary waking consciousness, we don't use it as often as we think. Did you ever drive your car while conversing with somebody at the same time? Try to recall an interesting conversation which engrossed you, and ask yourself how you managed to get to your destination. The necessary functions to get you there were all working: you saw the streets, the stop signs, and the lights; you turned the steering wheel and pressed on the gas and brakes in the correct ways; you reached your destination. However, you weren't quite aware of doing all these things, as you were focused on the conversation. You were driving in a habitual way, like an airplane on automatic pilot, not exercising free will. This happens all the time in various situations. We seem to be so absorbed in one thing that other things seem to occur with no thinking involved. Even the item that absorbs us may be occurring in a habitual way.

Let me show you how. Try doing this. As you continue reading this page, say to yourself, "I'm aware of myself sitting here reading this book." Try to focus on this self-awareness as you read. You may notice that after a while this awareness recedes into the background of your attention and that your reading proceeds in an automatic manner. Your conscious experiences, like your actions, seem to have a "mind of their own." Yet, it is this very ability to access and direct free will that is essential in dealing with psychological problems. It is the key to changing the pattern of your personality.

How do the readings of Edgar Cayce fit into all of this? Before answering this question, let's recapitulate what we've said so far. We see that personality consists of a unique organization or pattern of traits in dynamic interaction. Each trait in turn represents an individualistic expression of more basic elements interacting with each other and having "one foot," as it were, in subjectivity and the other in objectivity. This duality of characteristics is paradoxically countered by the unity of consciousness inherent in self-awareness, as traits spin around and express themselves through a central I-ness.

By way of analogy, imagine that you are a violin player and that the melody you are playing represents your personality. Each note represents one of your traits, while the relationship between them symbolizes your personality. Even if you played the melody in a different key, with a different instrument, or just hummed it for that matter, it would still be the same tune. The melody is unique, and you seem to like it, so you play it over and over. Sometimes you are aware of doing this, while at other times your mind is elsewhere, and you play habitually.

Now think of your own personality traits. What words best describe you? Focus on those traits that have been with you for a while, those that are enduring. It is such traits that the Cayce readings deal with. More significantly, they look at these traits within the bigger picture of reality.

Recall that the readings tell us that the basic building blocks of reality are spirit, mind, and will. Spirit is the essence of life, mind generates patterns, and will provides the direction for this. Patterns created by mind appear in different ways in different realities. In our world of ordinary consciousness, they relate to our personalities and incorporate both subjective and objective referents. A recurrent phrase in the readings that expresses this idea is "the spirit is the life, mind is the builder, and the physical is the result." This underscores the close relationship between the mind and objective reality. Moreover, as mind is the builder, it places the emphasis on waking consciousness as the primary focus of personality. This means that, even though we have an objective body, it is the mind that both fashions this body and simultaneously experiences it. Although a person can talk about his or her interests, values, attitudes, race, ethnic group, height, musical aptitude, compulsive gambling, bleeding ulcers, and myriad other personality descriptives, it is the psychological experience of these that counts. In other words, awareness is the bottom line of personality, whether this refers to elements of one's subjective world or to those of the objective world. The subjective world is the primary arena both of personality and personality change. Dealing with psychological problems, then, means using your mind in new, constructive ways. This, of course, means exercising one's will in certain ways. The readings tell us that, while free will is limited in life, we should access what we have. Moreover, if this is done in an appropriate manner, it will increase.

The Cayce model of personality is more intricate than that presented thus far. According to the readings, personality is not an isolated event. Just as personality is defined as a pattern, its structure relates to other patterns that are unconscious. There are many such patterns. One of these relates to childhood. Let's suppose that when you were a child you were traumatized by a near-drowning experience. As an adult you have absolutely no recollection of this, but it manifests itself as an intense fear of water. Telling you about it doesn't seem to help much, as you still maintain your phobia. The negative experience seems to have set up a memory pattern relating to the present hydrophobic condition. All childhood experiences, both positive and negative, influence present personality traits and determine what we sense, perceive, think, feel, act, and intuit, in addition to influencing our bodily processes and behavior.

A good way to understand these patterns is to look at them as if they were slides in a slide projector. Imagine many blank slides arranged in a row, one for every year of life. Make believe that the projection on the screen represents personality. At birth the screen is assumed to be blank, since nothing has yet been experienced. By the end of the first year, a rudimentary pattern is projected through the first slide, the one closest to the light bulb. Since light is passing through all the slides, whatever is etched on the first slide leaves a trace or "shadow" on all the other slides. This means that whatever is experienced after the first year is affected by that trace, so that by the end of the second year, the next slide would represent the cumulative effect of both years. This process continues throughout life until all slides are completed. To add to this analogy, make believe that certain experiences carry more weight than others and have a greater impact on the slides' imprint. In our example of the hydrophobic person, this means that his near-drowning experiences sensitized him to all future encounters with water. To complete the analogy, imagine that all the slides are enclosed in the projector and that the only thing visible is what is on the screen. This demonstrates that, although memory patterns are mostly forgotten, they are still very much alive in the unconscious mind.

The Cayce readings go beyond childhood, however, and assert that personality dynamically relates to other patterns acquired from previous lives as well as other levels of reality. The idea of reincarnation may present a problem for some people, as it goes against their belief systems. As we saw earlier, Edgar Cayce himself also had difficulty with this notion, and it took him a while to assimilate it into his Christian perspective. Interestingly, the readings do not make belief in reincarnation a sine qua non to benefit from their recommendations. Indeed, mere acceptance of reincarnation does not mean that psychological problems will go away, any more than the rejection of this notion means that they will stay. A person who discovers that he once lived during the reign of Louis XIV and created a personality pattern during that lifetime that is now causing emotional distress might derive some satisfaction at the level of intellectual curiosity, yet his problem still remains. Conversely, there are countless individuals who profess no belief in reincarnation and who experience significant improvement with their problems. This, of course, includes most people in Western society. Again, it is important to remember that, according to the readings, changes occur only when one makes constructive decisions and applies them.

In addition to reincarnation, the readings also discuss interim experiences that occur between lives. These involve "planetary sojourns" in which we experience different states of consciousness symbolized by the sun, moon, and the various planets of our solar system. As life is continuous, so too is consciousness. However, the quality of the experience varies. With earthly incarnations, psychological experience remains the same: subjectivity revolves around a self-awareness and is coordinated to an objective reality. The mental experiences between lives, however, is ineffable. They appear as latent or manifest urges during one's lifetime. The Cayce view of personality is thus multifaceted. It reflects patterns created on many levels of reality. One reading puts it like this:

> For, every experience in the mental world arises from the correlation of one incident with another or one's feelings from one period to another. 3212-1

To fully understand the Cayce view on personality we must look at the concept of *actualization*. It is here that psychological problems have their origins. Actualization means to make real, to make actual. According to the readings, there is a push or tendency in nature directed toward the realization of an end. Everything is growing and striving toward wholeness and completion. This is a process of spiritual becoming. Think of it like the blossoming of a spiritual essence. It can be seen everywhere in nature. An acorn actualizes its potential when it grows into an oak tree. The pattern of the oak tree is inherent in the acorn itself, and given the proper environment, it grows into a lovely tree. Actualization is also seen in the principle that "like begets like." This means that elements in nature, at all levels of reality, renew or regenerate themselves. The oak tree produces new acorns that produce new oak trees. The readings tell us that this "reproductive principle" expresses a basic spiritual law at the level of physical reality. Finally, and perhaps more immediate in concern, is the notion that the process of actualization is tied in to various regulatory devices that insure its end. This brings us to the concept of *karma*.

The readings often refer to karma when discussing reincarnation. One of the easiest ways to understand this is to think of it as unconscious memory. As we have seen, personality consists of a pattern that is dynamically related to other patterns. Karma helps us to understand how these patterns relate to each other, especially with regard to psychological disorders. An examination of the readings shows that they seem to follow certain unconscious laws. One such law reflects a balancing principle, a sort of "corrective device." This links present psychological dilemmas to previous patterns within a context of spiritual actualizing directives. Karma can be viewed as this equalizing tendency. Before examining this in greater detail, let's see how it works in the physical body.

Your body begins at conception as a one-celled organism, the zygote. The nucleus of this cell contains a genetic code or blueprint that determines the manner in which your characteristics can express themselves as you develop. Many predispositions are encoded in these genes. These include such physical traits as skin color, sex, height, and others, as well as tendencies toward various physical diseases. Also encoded are various psychological traits like temperament, leadership potential, and so on, as well as predispositions toward psychological disorders. The zygote has an inherent tendency to grow and develop into a mature adult. As it develops, this directive is mirrored throughout its cells in their regeneration and renewal. The body also utilizes various self-regulatory or balancing devices to effect its proper growth.

For example, the temperature of the body is usually 98.6. If, on a very warm day, your temperature should rise, the body automatically regulates itself by causing you to perspire. Perspiration acts as a coolant, enabling the temperature to fall. If your temperature should fall below its normal level, you begin to shiver. The resulting friction and heat cause the temperature to rise. This homeostatic device ensures that body temperature stays on course.

Suppose, however, that you have a high fever resulting from a viral infection. Here, the temperature represents an additional corrective device, the attempt of the body to burn the virus. A physician's advice that the fever has to run its course would be an expression of this. The physician might also recommend that you rest to prevent the situation from getting worse and that you take aspirin to feel more comfortable. He might also warn you to avoid certain foods during your illness, as they may precipitate a future, unrelated problem.

Now, it seems that you have certain choices here. You might be the type of person who doesn't like to take any kind of medication; so you decide to just take it easy for a while and accept the fact that you'll be feeling miserable. Or you might decide to rest but take aspirin to get some degree of relief. Or perhaps job obligations do not allow you to rest, so you go to work with your fever, debating whether or not to take aspirin. In addition, you also have a choice to make regarding the dietary recommendations of the doctor. With each of these options comes different consequences. These relate to the extent of your suffering, when you will recover, and whether or not you will have future complications. What you choose to do about your problem will create definite effects.

Let's stay with this idea some more and assume that your fever is due to a bacterial infection. Now the physician may prescribe some medication to knock out the illness. Again, he may recommend rest, aspirin, dietary restrictions, and so on, and again the outcome will be determined by your choices. Suppose that you do everything he tells you except diet. You get over your ailment, but six months later develop a gastrointestinal problem. Filled with regret for not following your doctor's advice, you return to him, and the process repeats itself.

What can we see here? First is the body's push toward actualization. Second is the homeostatic, balancing principle, the modus operandi toward this end. Third, and most important, are the choices one makes. Such choices affect the actualization process in many ways and by various degrees. Everything you do sets you up for some future contingency. In fact, *everything you think and do is going to produce some consequence.*

If you were to develop an interest in studying the biological functioning of the body, you would learn in time to identify certain factors that foster its growth. Choosing to work with these in constructive ways would not only keep you in tiptop shape but would also increase your longevity. Your decision to *work with the laws* of your body and to harmonize with its pattern would certainly pay off. You also would experience an increase in your degree of freedom. Isn't it true that you have fewer choices available to you if you're lying home sick in bed, or worse still, in some hospital room? A healthy body has more options in life. This may seem strange at first since the idea of "law" seems rigid and fixed. The truth of the matter, however, is quite the opposite. Working in harmony with natural laws on all levels of reality brings with it greater freedom.

Going beyond the physical body now, we can perhaps begin to understand the origins and purposes of emotional problems within the context of actualization. Simply put, if a tendency toward actualization exists everywhere in nature and the macrocosm is reflected in the microcosm, then the same principles we see in the physical body must also exist on a higher level of being. The readings refer to the *soul* as this being. They tell us that we are not bodies but rather souls. We each have a spiritual nature which is derived from God. Each of us is a miniature version of God and, as such, has an identity of oneness and wholeness with God. Yet, paradoxically, each also has an individual identity. The soul then knows itself to be itself, while simultaneously experiencing a oneness with God. It has a "part-within-a-whole" nature as it were. Like God, the soul consists of a creative source or spirit. Integrated with spirit is mind through which the soul expresses itself, and will, which directs this action. What does it mean when we say that the soul expresses itself? Perhaps it would be easier to understand this if you think of a Big I being at the center of your soul, just as your *little I* forms the basis of your personality. At the level of the little I, self-expression is a way of defining one's personality. This can be seen in many aspects of life, from one's dress, cars, hobbies, careers, friends, and so on. The same occurs with the Big I. It constantly seeks to define itself. Self-expression, at any level of reality, is guided by a pattern or model expressed by God. This divine pattern reflects the creativity of spirit and is based in oneness and love. The ideal self-expression of the Big I represents a variation of this pattern. Like a melody is a variation of a musical theme, the variation of the divine theme reflects harmony, system, and balance. It is complementary to God's pattern. It is also unique. Just as human identity is unique through one's fingerprint, the ideal pattern expressed by the Big I defines its "soul print." The more the Big I seeks to express its ideal self, the more it reflects its part-within-a-whole nature, or defines its *individuality*. The readings tell us that:

> Individuality is that which shines out from within, separating one from another. Though one may be but a dot, that dot remains ever individual . . . yet a portion of the whole. The nearer one becomes to that which will give its *individuality* —yet losing itself in the whole—the *more* individuality one attains! 345-2

Individuality is in a continuous process of becoming or actualizing. Its expression can occur on any level of reality. At the human level, it expresses itself through such higher traits as love, mercy, patience, long-suffering, hope, faith, peace, trust, and others. To see this more clearly, return for a moment to the earlier analogy of the slide projector. Imagine that there is a "master slide" built into the projector and that this slide is a pattern of a snowflake. Since all light projected on the screen passes through this master slide, its etchings affect all other slides. The pattern of the snowflake reflects a higher order of things, one of wholeness and trans-personal values. This represents your individuality in the bigger picture of things. Just as one snowflake is different from all others, so too is your individuality unique; and just as there is a commonality between all snow-flakes, this individuality reflects a oneness underlying everything in life.

The expressions of the Big I in its journey through mind define the *entity*. Having free will, the Big I can express itself any way it chooses. The more aligned it is with the divine pattern, the more it manifests its individuality. As it deviates from this pattern, individuality becomes less defined. Such deviation results when the Big I interferes with the pattern, creating changes and mutations in its form. It also occurs when the Big I identifies itself with these alterations in pattern. All deviations produce a weakening in the connection of the Big I with God, in the identity of being part-within-a-whole. More and more, self-identification consolidates around the "part." To correct these "errors," the divine pattern sets into motion various corrective maneuvers, putting the Big I back on target. This is karma.

The Big I can go off course on any level of reality, spiritual, mental, or physical. On the human level, all prior patterns of actions and corrective reactions are expressed through one's mind and body. This can take place in a latent or hidden manner, as well as in a more overt way. Negative karma may come across as physical and mental disorders, accidents, poverty, and in many other ways. In the same manner, good fortune in one's life may be related to positive karma.

Human self-awareness, or the little I, is the only link one has to the Big I. For most people, the little I does not directly experience the unity of its consciousness with God, only its own part-nature, or separateness. The expression of this separateness relates to the way the readings define *personality*. They tell us that personality reflects the masks that people wear to enhance themselves and further their self-interests. These include such "lower" traits as envy, doubt, stubbornness, self-righteousness, self-consciousness, hostility, greed, jealousy, and many others. The readings refer to such traits as "self-aggrandizing."

While personality and individuality are not usually in harmony with each other, the degree of incongruence varies from person to person. Any one trait can serve to reinforce a sense of separateness or to enhance oneness. For instance, if an artist creates beautiful paintings for the fame and fortune they bring her, she would be emphasizing her ego and separateness as a human being. If, however, she paints for the sake of aesthetic expression and uplifts others through her work, her personality would be more in line with her individuality.

Let's return to the analogy of the violin player to understand this more clearly. Recall that the melody of the violinist represents his personality. Assume that he plays this tune repeatedly. Now let's place him in an orchestra that is performing a symphony, an orchestra where the conductor is invisible. Our violinist soon becomes aware of certain things. First, he feels a special bond with the other musicians. Regardless of whether they are playing clarinets, trumpets, or any other instruments, they share in his musical creativity. His self-awareness seems to be expanding and embracing these other musicians. This can be likened to the awakening of the Big I. Then there's the symphony itself. The violinist realizes that his melody doesn't harmonize too well with it. It somehow seems out of place. He also sees that he can modify it into a beautiful score for violin that will fit in perfectly with the symphony. It will be a variation on its theme. The violin score can be likened to the ideal definition of the Big I, while the actualization of this expresses its individuality. The violinist now has to make a decision. He can choose to ignore the symphony and continue to play his favorite melody. Or, he can decide to modify his melody into a score for violin, so that it flows with the symphony. In essence, he can continue to emphasize his personality and separateness or choose to radiate his individuality. All the while he wonders who composed this marvelous symphony and who is conducting it.

How does all this relate to psychological disorders. The answer lies in the goal of the Big I. Just as the body expresses itself from the moment of its conception through its growth and development, so too does the Big I seek an ideal expression of itself. Each of us has an inborn, inherent push in this direction. Fully developed, the actualized person would be forever changed, as individuality permeates personality. This is the process of personality transformation and spiritual becoming. It is ongoing and occurs in all dimensions of reality.

Now the *little I* can help or hinder this process through the exercise of its will. Although free will is inherent in the soul, its accessibility increases as one expresses the ideal of the Big I. In doing this, one is working with the laws of nature rather than against them, and as we saw earlier, this goes hand in hand with greater freedom. Ultimate freedom resides in individuality and is more restricted in personality. Despite this, the little I is strong enough to direct the expression and definition of the Big I. It can foster or hinder its actualization. Helping the process means aligning one's personality traits in a spiritual direction. Imbalance occurs to the extent that personality is egocentric or selfish.

It is this very imbalance that relates to psychological disorders. In effect, such problems reflect the consequences of actions taken at some previous point in time. Just as the body makes homeostatic corrections when it is off balance, so too is the path of the Big I readjusted when it is off course. Both kinds of corrections represent the operation of karma, which is inherent in the divine pattern. All this takes place at the level of the unconscious mind and, as such, we are unaware of it. We are very much aware, however, of its effects. These can represent a moment in one's life or an entire lifetime. They can be seen in our good times, as well as in our misfortunes.

Now how does this work? How does a psychological problem relate to a divine restoration of balance? Let's look at this by considering the spiritual concept of love, and assume that one expression of this in personality is through altruistic behavior. Altruism means caring for others, and helping them for no reason other than to assure their welfare. Suppose that at a certain point in your soul's development you acted in a very selfish manner. You were conceited and viewed others as inferior. You associated only with people who could serve your ego in some manner. Although you felt good about yourself and were happy with life, the pattern of your personality was incongruent with that of your individuality. Unconsciously you were setting yourself up for a future problem. That problem appears in your present life as a social phobia. At this point in time, you describe yourself as extremely shy. You avoid social situations out of fear of embarrassment and humiliation or else endure them with a great deal of discomfort. You can't understand why you are like this. You might blame your parents and the way they brought you up or look to other environmental factors. You might even assume that you were genetically predisposed to become phobic. The Cayce readings would not disagree with these interpretations but would go far deeper. Look at how one reading expresses this:

> Environs and hereditary influences are much deeper than that which is ordinarily conceded in the psychology of the present day. For the environs and the hereditary influences are spiritual as well as physical, and are physical because of the spiritual application of the abilities of the entity in relationship to spiritual development. 852-12

Notice here how one's present personality pattern relates to the degree of progress toward "spiritual development." What mediates between an imbalance incurred on some level of development and your present problem is difficult to say. It can take a variety of paths, encompassing spiritual, mental, and physical parameters. The socially phobic individual, for example, may choose to incarnate in a family where both parents have the same problem, and thereby pick it up from them. Or he may have normal parents, but suffer an injury in childhood which predisposes him for the phobia. Or it may simply exist as an unconscious tendency that is triggered off by an external situation at some point in his development. The thing to understand here is that the incongruity between individuality and personality represents a conflict within a *system* of body, mind, and spirit. Body can be going in one direction, mind in another, and spirit in a third! A psychological disorder is an expression of such a conflict. Although the problem can be centered in any one of these components, because of their interdependence, the entire system is affected.

To help clarify this idea, make believe that your body is a radio. Further, imagine that high frequency radio waves represent spiritual patterns, while low frequency waves are mental patterns. Your ordinary consciousness can be likened to the radio being turned on, representing an interaction of the radio waves with the radio. If the radio has a mechanical defect, what comes out will be garbled. Similarly, if you have a problem with your body, it may come across as a psychological disturbance like anxiety, depression, or in other ways. In such cases the problem can be considered as a mental reaction to the biological event. Since the problem is centered in the body, treatment would be physical in nature, much like a broken radio would be repaired. If the biological condition is corrected, the psychological problem will go away, in the same way that the radio will play well once it's fixed. But suppose that the radio isn't broken. In this situation, a garbled message would represent a problem in the radio waves. High frequency waves may be interfering with low frequency waves. Similarly, some psychological problems are centered in spiritual and/or mental factors as experienced in ordinary consciousness. In these cases, treatment would address psychospiritual concerns. Now make believe that there's a problem with both the radio and the radio waves. With psychological disorders, this is usually the case. This means that they are multifaceted and reflect spiritual, mental, and physical factors, all of which need to be addressed. They represent not only disruptive patterns of psychological functioning originating within the mind itself, but also mental reactions to other patterns rooted in unconscious spiritual and mental sources, as well as those related to the body's physiology. This is the basis of Cayce's holistic treatment approach.

Let's illustrate this with a hypothetical case of depression. Suppose you were to badly burn your face. Now while the burn itself is a physical event, your pain is a mental reaction to it. If, in addition to the pain, you begin to brood over the appearance of your face, you would be causing another physical event, namely, the retardation of your body's healing process. This, in turn, would produce additional mental reactions of frustration, hopelessness, and low self-esteem. Finally, these feelings would instigate a spiritual reaction which would come across as guilt. Low self-esteem, hopelessness, and guilt are all symptoms of depression. So what starts out as a burn winds up as a psychological disorder! Such an interplay of factors highlights the usual complexity inherent in emotional problems.

As you can see, the equalizing tendency of the divine pattern, while originating from a simple basis of actualization, can appear in many different and interrelated ways. As psychological problems are thus complex, what can be done about them? Can you really change your mind? Certainly you can. The purpose of this book is to help you to understand the nature of your problem and its causes and how to deal with it in the most effective manner. Let's continue now by examining how the Cayce readings tie in with some of the popular theoretical models of today's psychology.

3

Are Psychological Disorders Bad Habits?

We break a habit by forming a habit. This we all do.
                                    Edgar Cayce reading 3287-2
The mental or habit forming is of the subconscious . . .
                                    Edgar Cayce reading 137-127

The multifaceted approach of the Cayce material links the causes of psychological disorders to a variety of factors, with symptoms appearing as psychological, biological, or behavioral events, or, more usually, as a combination of these. It is not unreasonable, then, to find the information in the readings related in some way to the major orientations of contemporary psychology.

One such perspective is Freud's psychoanalysis. Freud has had a major impact on twentieth-century thinking. From his model comes the view of unconscious causation. Psychological disorders are seen as originating from repressed conflicts of childhood, revolving around

sexuality and aggression. While the readings acknowledge the importance of these feelings, they do not see
them the way Freud does. Moreover, the readings tell us
that, although childhood conflicts can, indeed, play a
significant role in the etiology of mental problems, other
related causes must be addressed. These include physiological as well as spiritual factors. One reading puts it
like this:

> In analyzing the mind and its reactions, oft indi-
> viduals who would psychoanalyze or who would in-
> terpret the reactions that individual entities take,
> leave out those premises of soul, mind, body.
>
> As we would give, an entity body-mind was first a
> soul before it entered into material consciousness.
> 4083-1

In addition to omitting spiritual and physiological factors, the readings also point out that psychoanalytic interpretations often lead people into believing what
they're told about their problem. As this explanation is
assimilated into the individual's belief system, it not only
fails to solve the problem but creates new ones. This can
be seen in the following case, where a man asked the
sleeping Cayce if his problem was caused by some childhood fear, as he had been told by psychoanalysts. The
reading comments:

> As we find, there are disturbing conditions, but
> these to a great extent have arisen from the fear that
> has been created by what the body has been told is
> the source of his disturbance. Don't believe 'em!
> 3318-1

This individual came to Cayce for help with an anxiety disorder and was told that his problem got worse be-

cause of his therapy. Although the readings disagreed with the limited approach of psychoanalytic theory, they did not undermine the significant contribution it made to the role of unconscious determinants in personality functioning. This can be seen in the advice given to one individual when he asked how he could be of service to others:

> Study in those fields and with those associates in which such activities may be gained. Study Freud, study astrological aspects, study numerology. 1595-1

The importance of Freud is apparent here. However, by including him within the esoteric approaches of astrology and numerology, the readings are addressing a larger picture of reality in which human personality is but one expression. Especially significant in Freud, as well as in the readings, is the emphasis on dream interpretation as an invaluable aid in self-understanding.

Another model in contemporary psychology looks at psychological problems as physiological problems. This is the biological approach. Here, both causes and treatments are physical in nature. Whether the problem is a phobia, amnesia, multiple personality, alcoholism, male erectile dysfunction, indeed, any emotional problem at all, it is basically a physical condition. While the readings agree that physiological factors play a role in psychological conditions, they always correlate these with spiritual and mental contributions.

From the humanistic theory in psychology comes the concept of actualization. It is here that healthy psychological development is seen as the successful development of a personality potential inherent at birth. Like the seed of a flower, this needs a nourishing environment in order to flourish. Psychological problems occur to the extent that such an environment is unavailable. Since humanistic theory views actualization only from the perspective of personality, it is limited, according to the readings, where actualization relates to the spiritual unfolding of individuality. In addition, this model fails to address the role of physiological factors in psychological disorders.

The model with one of the closest ties to the Cayce readings is existential psychology. This perspective emphasizes our primary need to understand the ultimate meaning of being human and to develop a satisfying rationale and foundation for existence. Questions dealing with the origin and destiny of humankind are fundamental to personality formation. Psychological disorders relate to existential frustration, guilt, and anxiety. The biggest drawback of this model is in its failure to address physiological factors in emotional problems.

A final model which we'll look at is the transpersonal perspective. This also fits in very well with the Cayce viewpoint as it considers reality to be multidimensional and assumes the existence of a higher self. This self is impersonal and nonjudgmental and reflects such principles as love, altruism, creativity, intuition, higher meaning, purpose, ethics, and values. In contrast to this is the ego, or the personality one identifies with. Psychological problems are viewed as incongruities between the ego and the higher spiritual order of things. The drawback of the transpersonal model is that it doesn't note the contribution of physiological factors to psychological conditions.

While this brief overview fails to do justice to the complexities of these models, it does illustrate their relationship to the information in the readings, as well as their limitations relative to the Cayce approach. Their similarities to Cayce lie more in the area of causes rather than treatments. The readings agree that humanity needs a meaningful rationale for existence, that this existence is transpersonal and includes spiritual factors, that unconscious as well as physiological factors play vital roles in psychological disorders, and that actualization is a paramount issue in life. The readings also agree with some of the therapeutic approaches of these models. This is especially seen in the use of dreams, hypnosis, visualization, and other techniques, and of course in the use of physical intervention.

The one theory which comes closest to the Cayce viewpoint on treatment, as well as its explanation of the immediate causes of psychological disorders, is the behavioral model. Ironically, this model also makes various assumptions of human nature that are most discrepant from those of the readings. Behavioral theory tells us that psychological problems originate in faulty patterns of learning, especially those that occur during childhood. It emphasizes the concept of *habit* and sees personality as very mechanical in nature. It is not too concerned with causes, focusing instead on solutions. Solutions, in turn, are contingent on specific actions taken by the individual. It is here that the model fits well with the Cayce readings, for they too emphasize action and application.

The readings also see personality as habitual in many ways. Remember, however, that they see psychological problems as conflicts in a system involving personality and individuality. It is here that the behavioral model is quite opposite to the Cayce position. The focus of behavioral theory is on objective reality. It does not address spiritual issues. It views human beings as automatons, with no decision-making capabilities. Psychological problems are maladaptive patterns resulting from poor conditioning rather than poor choices. They are "bad habits" and can be changed to more adaptive patterns through strategies of relearning or reconditioning.

The behavioral perspective has two lines of origin. The first is based on the famous experiments conducted by the Russian physiologist Pavlov. Working with simple re-flexes, Pavlov found that he could teach an animal to re-spond in a brand-new way to some stimulus. To see how this works, imagine that you have a dog at home. Now, what does the dog do when you feed it? Among other things, it salivates. This is a natural, inborn response. If the telephone should ring, however, the dog would not salivate. Now imagine what would occur if you fed the dog every time the telephone rang. After a while, it would probably salivate as soon as it heard the phone! Since dogs don't normally salivate when phones ring, we would have to assume that this reaction was learned. This is basically what Pavlov discovered, and he called it a conditioned response. His theory of *respondent conditioning* helps us to see how certain psychological prob-lems can be acquired.

Let's suppose, for example, that you get stuck in an el-evator for several hours and become very frightened. The next time you go into an elevator, you respond with the same fear. You have acquired elements of a phobia or, in Pavlov's terms, a conditioned fear response. The principles of respondent conditioning have been ap-plied in the treatment of a variety of psychological disor-ders.

The other line of origin for the behavioral model is known as *operant conditioning* and is based on the well-known work of Skinner. Skinner showed us that the for-mation of a habit depends on the consequences we encounter in a given situation. Since consequences are either rewards or punishments, what this means is that if behavior is followed by positive events, it stays with us, and if it's followed by negative events, it does not. If you stay away from elevators because you got stuck in one, you will in essence be rewarding yourself by avoiding the fear. This pattern continues into a full-blown phobia. Like respondent conditioning, Skinner's theory has also given us many strategies to cope with emotional problems.

The behavioral theories have produced many derivatives. One of these is the *cognitive-behavioral* model, a mixture of behavioral and cognitive approaches. The emphasis here is on the person's thought processes during the formation of a habit. This is something which both respondent and operant conditioning do not highlight, focusing instead on behavioral events. In contrast, the cognitive-behavioral approach views behavior as closely related to a person's interpretation of the situation encountered. In other words, our actions depend on how we see things, rather than being automatic responses to stimuli. What may be seen as threatening to me may not be so for you. There are many cognitive-behavioral coping techniques available to deal with psychological problems. For simplicity, the generic term *behavioral* will be used throughout to refer to both behavioral and cognitive-behavioral approaches.

Let's return to the readings now. The Cayce material, by expanding the concept of habit well beyond immediate causes, presents a more complex picture. The habit becomes a focal point of interacting spiritual, mental, and physical patterns within an ongoing conflict between personality and individuality. These patterns interface with the physical body at birth and can predispose the individual to psychological problems at any point in life. Whether or not they occur depends on the interplay of such predispositions with a variety of environmental factors as well as with the use of one's will. The manner of habit expression varies. It can be centered in the mind, body, or spirit, and since these interact, all three are involved.

Those readings which center the psychological problem in the body emphasize functional and/or structural malfunctions. These include incoordinations in the nervous system, glandular imbalances, disturbances in circulation, and many other factors. McMillin[1] notes an interesting dichotomy that the readings make in the physiological correlates of psychological disorders. A difference is made between a state of "dis-ease," and that of "disease." When a psychological problem is the disease state, it is less severe, as no physical pathology is present. This can be likened to having a bad cold. Although it can affect your daily activities, it produces no major upheavals in life. Many of the conditions referred to as neurotic disorders or personality disorders would fit well here. When an emotional problem is considered a disease, however, the imbalance in the system reaches a point where physical pathology is evident. What all this means is that a maladaptive habit pattern can have various degrees of physiological malfunction associated with it, and this, of course, has implications for how it is corrected.

When the readings center the psychological problem within the mind, they focus on various destructive attitudes and behavior patterns held by the individual. When spiritual factors are addressed, the higher ideals of the person are questioned. Because body, mind, and spirit interact, the total picture of the habit patterns usually represents a combination of all three.

In addition to broadening the view of habit, the readings also tell us that it actually originates with desire. This can be seen in the following comments:

> Do ye know what longings and desires create, that are only gratifying the emotions of the body? and how they become as hangers-on in the form of habits that may undermine? 2269-1

The reason that habits become "hangers-on" is that they take root in the subconscious mind. This is yet another way in which the readings differ from the behavioral model, where this is viewed as nonexistent. Despite these differences between behavioral psychology and the Cayce readings, they agree for the most part on how a maladaptive habit is expressed and on how to treat it. Each model sees a habit as a learned, automatic reaction occurring in some situation. This reaction incorporates a psychological component, which relates to what's going on inside your head: the things you say to yourself, your feelings and wishes, your fantasies and daydreams—all of these make up the mental expression of the habit. The habit also has a behavioral component. This represents the things that you do: what you talk about, whom you associate with, the sports you play, and so on. As we have seen, the Cayce model also adds a physiological expression of the habit which refers to the things that are happening within your body, like your heartbeat, blood pressure, breathing, digestion, and other such processes. Let's look at an example of this from the Cayce perspective. Suppose a man is afraid of flying. As he lies in bed one night anticipating a morning business flight, his fears show up as psychological and physiological patterns. He agonizes over the flight and desperately tries to find the courage that everything will be all right. As he pictures himself strapped in the seat of the plane, he hears the rumbling noises it makes on takeoff. His heart races, as he rushes to catch his breath. He tries to focus his attention on the possibility of a last-minute cancellation and, in so doing, drifts into sleep.

The same habit pattern occurs the next day, with the addition of a behavioral component. This can be seen as he stammers at the baggage check. He also smokes one cigarette after another while waiting to board. He mechanically turns the pages of his newspaper. All the while, his mind and body are in high gear. A last-minute phone call from his boss, informing him that the trip is canceled, results in tremendous relief.

If psychological disorders are maladaptive habits, how can they be handled? Both behavioral psychology and the readings agree that action and application are needed to effect change in one's life. In the behavioral model, actions are aimed at habit change through reconditioning the individual. Techniques include a variety of treatment approaches subsumed under such therapies as behavior modification, behavior therapy, cognitive-behavioral therapy, and others. All of these have produced self-management strategies, which will be considered here.

There are two basic approaches to self-help. The first allots an active role to psychological processes and helps you to change by working directly with your mind. You can do this by altering any component of the habitual mental pattern, like your thoughts or feelings. The airplane phobic, for instance, can learn to identify and dispute his irrational beliefs or other thinking distortions related to flying. Or he can teach himself to be calm whenever he imagines himself flying. Working with the mind can also entail a restructuring of the entire mental pattern. Here, the phobic can learn a brand-new fantasy where flying is experienced in a very positive manner. You may be wondering at this point if such strategies can really help. Can changes in mental events really produce changes in real events? Behavioral psychologists tell us that they can, and the readings concur. Since mind is the builder, whatever we dwell on in consciousness is eventually expressed in physical reality.

One doesn't have to be limited to this approach, however. Since habits also express themselves through behavior, a second strategy is to deal with them at this level. The airplane phobic can work with his habit by learning new behavior patterns in real-life situations. He can, for example, learn to associate flying with various rewarding experiences, surround himself with pleasant situations related to flying, or use many other techniques. Here, the psychological problem is approached by focusing on overt actions in specific situations, rather than on psychological mediating processes. The readings also agree with the value of this strategy.

As both strategies result in change, let's now consider what actually happens here. The behavioral model tells us that old habits are unraveled, and that stimuli which previously produced negative reactions now produce positive ones. In the case of the airplane phobic, this means that his fear of airplanes is now extinguished and is replaced with a more adaptive response. The readings disagree with this interpretation of change. They tell us that old habits never become extinguished. Instead, new ones are formed, which become embedded in the personality. What this means is that an old habit cannot be broken but only substituted with a new one. It can't be wiped out the way chalkmarks can be erased from a chalkboard. Instead, new markings have to be made on the chalkboard.

To clarify this, let's assume that you are right-handed, and that someone offers you a big reward if you learn to use you left hand, instead of your right one. You agree to this, and begin training your left hand in writing skills. After a while, the "old habit" of right-handedness is replaced with the "new habit" of left-handedness, with your left hand in control. Obviously, you still have the ability to use your right hand but refrain from doing so. In a similar vein, the habitual pattern of the psychological disorder is associated with emotional pain, and as a new pattern relinquishes that pain, it takes over the old one.

As the readings see a physiological component to the habit, they also address this issue when considering habit change. When the psychological disorder has the status of dis-ease, the therapeutics are non-specific, or more general in nature. In addition to fostering a healing process, they are also preventative and ensure against relapse, or a deterioration of the situation. Because they are general, these therapeutics are applicable to anyone, sick or well. They include working with diet, exercise, osteopathy, hydrotherapy, medicine, and various mechanical appliances. They aim to improve circulation, assimilation, relaxation, and elimination. When the psychological problem reaches the level of disease, the goals are basically the same, although the readings are much more specific with physical therapeutics.

The kinds of problems we'll be looking at in the following chapters are of the less severe type. While we will not be focusing on their physiological correlates, this is an area which should not be overlooked, as it is a significant aspect of the Cayce therapeutics. There are many excellent sources that expand on this for the interested reader to pursue (e.g., McGarey,[2] McMillin,[3] Mein,[4] and Reilly and Brad[5]).

The readings also tell us that habits are rooted in the subconscious mind. While this is not assumed in behavioral psychology, it will be considered here, as the readings often mention "suggestive therapeutics" as part of a treatment regimen.

Finally, the readings highlight the importance of placebo factors. These refer to the individual's expectations about the effectiveness of a procedure. The more one assumes that something positive will happen, the greater is the likelihood that this will occur. This, again, can be seen in the premise of the readings that mind is the builder.

Although there are differences between Cayce and the behavioral model in dealing with habits, the similarities outweigh them. Both emphasize a need for action and application. In addition, behavioral coping strategies are very amenable to the psychospiritual recommendations of the readings. I use the term psychospiritual because the readings always give psychological recommendations within a spiritual context. They emphasize a need to work with spiritual ideals, something that we'll examine in detail later on.

Let's now look at some of the specific coping strategies in dealing with maladaptive habits. The majority of these come from behavioral psychology, while a few have their origins in other schools of thought. Similarities of all techniques to the Cayce paradigm will be noted throughout. We'll first begin by examining a way of analyzing psychological problems, and then get into specifics with regard to strategies.

One final note needs to be addressed here. While the coping strategies presented in this book have been shown to be effective for the types of problems we'll be looking at, there is no way you can be certain that they will definitely work for you. It's important, then, to keep in mind that you may need help beyond these techniques. This, of course, includes professional counseling.

PART 2

▲

PSYCHOLOGICAL
SELF-HELP
TECHNIQUES

4

Analyzing Your Problem

Each day before retiring, make a résumé—not just mentally but upon paper—of what have been the *experiences* of the whole day. Edgar Cayce reading 830-3

The first thing you have to do in dealing with psychological disorders is to define the problem. For example, if you are depressed, what does this mean? In addition to feeling a certain way, you might also have various motives related to your depression, particular ways of looking at the world around you, specific ways of thinking about things, and many different kinds of behavior patterns. Each of these defines a specific symptom that relates to the overall problem. The best way to appreciate the nature of these symptoms is to write them down. Writing helps one to focus and also provides an organized manner of making daily changes in life. As a pre-

liminary step, try keeping notes for one day on every way your problem comes across. For depression, you might indicate that you felt very depressed upon awakening in the morning, that you were unable to concentrate on what you were doing at work, that you told a friend about your mood, that you ate more than usual at dinner, that you had a difficult time sleeping that night, and so on. This is an important first step in habit change and must be carried out with care. Regardless of the nature of the problem, such an analysis shows the extent to which it permeates your life on a daily basis.

Now look over your notes and try to recall where you were when each symptom appeared. Write this down as well. Continuing with depression, you might note that you were in bed in the morning, you were sitting at your desk at work, you were on the bus when talking to your friend, you were in the kitchen having dinner with your family, you were in the family room attempting to sleep at night, and so on. These are environmental factors and can be very useful tools in dealing with psychological problems.

Next, go over your notes again and write down what happened after each symptom occurred. What did you do after you woke up? What followed your concentration difficulties at work? How did your friend react when you told him of your depression? How did you feel when you overate? What did you think about during your evening insomnia? These are the consequences of your symptoms. Like environmental factors, they can play an important role in your attempts to manage your psychological disorder. Consequences refer to the rewards and punishments associated with the expression of the problem.

Rewards and punishments can relate to external events, internal events, or both. Rewarding consequences are those things that generally make you feel good. This will happen if you get something that you like.

Social support shown through compassion and understanding when you are depressed is an example of this and represents an external reward. An internal reward, on the other hand, refers to positive mental experiences that you entertain. Imagining the interest and attention that would come your way because of your depression would be an example of this. Rewarding experiences also occur when things that you dislike are taken away. An external reward here might be getting out of overtime work because of your depression, while an internal reward might be fantasizing the avoidance of a dreaded social engagement.

Punishing consequences are things that make you feel bad. This would take place if negative events occur or if positive ones are taken away, and again, they could be external, internal, or both. An example of a bad occurrence would be weight gain due to your depression. This is an external event. An internal event of the same kind would be ruminating about the dread of gaining weight. You might also feel bad if positive things in your life were removed because of your depression. This could happen externally if people began avoiding you or internally if you obsessed and worried about it.

After you have completed your notes, read them over carefully and make any additions, deletions, and corrections that are needed. At this point you are ready to prepare a *problem analysis list*. This list will indicate the various ways in which your symptoms come across, where you are when they appear, and what happens after they occur. Divide a piece of paper into six columns and write each event on a separate line. The first column should be headed *antecedants* and would include the situational factors related to the expression of the symptom. Things like location, time, other people, and items of this sort are included here. The next three columns should indicate the way in which you express the symptom. Head column two *thoughts* and include here all the perceptual and cognitive manifestations of the problem: how you see the world around you, what you say to yourself, and what you believe, daydream, and fantasize. The third column is to include the motives and feelings related to your problem, and should be headed *feelings*. Things like anxiety, sadness, helplessness, fatigue, lethargy, hunger, lack of interest, and other emotions and desires are put here. Label the fourth column *behaviors* and include the things you do that express your problem, like how you interact with other people, what you talk about, your nonverbal behavior, and things like this. In the fifth column, indicate the various rewards associated with the problem, and in the sixth, the punishments. Label these columns *rewards* and *punishments*, respectively.

Continuing with the example of depression, a person might indicate that he was on the bus going home from work (antecedant), when he began thinking about how worthless he was (thought), and felt very sad (feeling). He told his friend about this (behavior) and was given reassurance that things would get better (reward). Take your time here, as this list is an integral part of the self-management procedure you will employ.

The next step in analyzing your problem is to decide what you want to work on first. Look over your problem analysis list and see what part of the problem is easiest to deal with. Whether it's a thought, feeling, or behavior, pick a simple thing to start with, as this is usually more successful. If you begin with a difficult aspect of the problem, or attempt to do too many things at once, you'll probably fail. This can be likened to a person who makes several resolutions on New Year's Eve, only to follow through on none of them.

Once you've made your decision here, determine how often your symptom occurs. This is called *self-monitor-*

ing. It allows you to establish a base rating from which you can figure out what changes you'd like. What often happens when people monitor themselves is that they become more motivated to change. This occurs because they can see more clearly the extent of their problems. A person who wants to stop drinking, for example, may not realize how much he or she drinks until it is monitored. To monitor yourself, check on the frequency of the symptom during the day. For instance, if your problem is hypochondriasis and you decide to work on your verbal expression of this, determine a way of measuring how many times a day you talk to people about your fears of illness. You can do a frequency count in many ways, from using a golf counter, making notes on a pad, and the like. If you decide to work on your thoughts and feelings, then you may want to look at how much time they are with you.

The next thing you want to do is to define your *goal*. What changes do you want to see? What level of success would be satisfactory for you. For example, suppose you have a handwashing compulsion. Self-monitoring shows that this occurs on the average of fifty times a day, and you feel that a reduction to twenty times would be very beneficial. Your goal then would be set at this level. If your problem is nervousness and you see that you spend about seven hours a day like this, you may set one hour as your goal. Goal setting should be as realistic as possible. After doing this, decide on which coping strategy you want to use. These strategies will be described in the next chapter in sufficient detail to enable you to apply them.

After looking over the various coping techniques and deciding which one you are going to use, write out a *contract* for yourself. The word contract usually brings to mind an agreement between people that is enforceable in some way. Here, a contract refers to an agreement that you are making with yourself, with the intention that it too will be enforced. The elements of the contract will include the part of the problem that you are dealing with, its base rating, your goals, and the specific coping strategy that you will use. Are you dealing with a mental aspect of your problem or a behavioral component? How often does it occur in your daily life? What level of success would be satisfactory to you? How are you going to achieve your goals? The answers to these questions all become part of your contract. The contract should be written out with care and be as realistic as possible. Remember that it is better to begin with more feasible aspects of your problem, those that you can work on patiently. You might also set up some reward for yourself, contingent upon the successful fulfillment of the contract. A woman working with dieting, for instance, may agree to buy herself a new outfit once she loses weight.

Let's now consider specific self-help strategies that can be used in dealing with psychological disorders. As mentioned earlier, nearly all these techniques are derived from behavioral psychology, while a few have their roots in other models. All can be reconciled with Cayce's treatment recommendations. You will notice that some techniques are more effective with certain types of problems than others. Also, while each strategy may be used alone, in many cases a combination of techniques may prove more efficacious. These are some of the factors that you will have to consider in designing your contract. Later on, when we examine the Cayce material on working with ideals, we will again see the benefit of working with contracts.

5

Learning to Relax

Concentration upon relaxation is the greater or better manner for *any* body to relax. That is, *see* the body *relaxing, consciously* . . . as to let all of the tension, all of the strain, flow *out* of self—and find the body giving—giving—away.

Edgar Cayce reading 404-6

*One of the most effective ways of dealing with many psy-*chological disorders is *learning to relax.* I emphasize the word learning, to contrast specific coping skills with the many ordinary activities that people find relaxing and rewarding. What relaxes you? Perhaps it is doing garden work, or reading a good book, or doing aerobics. There are many relaxing activities. If there is nothing like this in your life, it is important that you find something, as the rewards are well worth the effort. Relaxation is an antidote to anxiety. Since many psychological problems have an inherent anxiety component, the value of relaxation lies in the creation of a new habit pattern that replaces this anxiety with a more positive reaction. In addition, relaxing activities are distracting so that less time is spent worrying about things.

Learning to relax as a coping skill uses a different approach. What it basically involves is a systematic program of teaching yourself to quiet your mind and body in a progressive, step-by-step manner. What's going on with your mind and body when you're not relaxed? Isn't it true that your body is aroused and that your mind is running rampant? The trick in learning to relax is to teach yourself to inhibit this activity. All systematic relaxation requires persistence, consistence, and patience.

Relaxation can be used as a coping strategy whenever the psychological problem has an anxiety component. This includes, of course, all the anxiety disorders. Anxiety, however, is also present in many other emotional disorders. These include, but are not limited to, mood disorders, conversion disorders, somatoform disorders, sexual disorders, and addictive disorders. To determine if you are a candidate for relaxation training, see if any of the symptoms you've chosen to work with include nervousness, worry, anxiety, apprehension, and other such feelings. There are many strategies here derived. They come from behavioral psychology, as well as from other models.

A popular relaxation procedure developed by Jacobson[1] is *progressive muscle relaxation.* This technique is actually based on a very simple idea. Try to remember how you felt the last time you stretched. Isn't it true that immediately afterwards, your body was very relaxed? This is the basis of progressive muscle relaxation. The only difference here is that you do this in a systematic way. This is an easy technique to learn. What you have to do is to tense certain muscles in your body for a few seconds, focus on the sensations you experience, relax these muscles, and again focus on the sensations. Begin by making yourself comfortable in a chair or in a bed. Now tense the muscles in your left hand by making a tight fist. Hold it for a while, and notice how the sensations of tension are becoming uncomfortable. Focus on these sensations. Now open up your hand, and let it relax. As your hand loosens up, notice the sensations of relaxation replacing those of tension. Do the same exercise with your right hand, and then proceed to tighten your biceps, shrug your shoulders, bring your head forward, bring it back, wrinkle your brow, tighten your eyes, clench your teeth, arch your back, tighten your abdomen, and stretch your legs. Each muscle group should be done one at a time, and in succession. Every time you tense up, hold it for a few seconds, and focus on the discomfort. When you let go, pay attention to the relaxation, and how good it feels. It would be beneficial if you record your procedure on tape. This way you can follow your own instructions as you proceed. Persistence, consistency, and patience are all ingredients for success. Do this once a day, and after a few weeks, you may notice that it becomes easier to relax. At this point try doing this. Without tensing and relaxing any muscles, just focus on them, and think that they are relaxing. Let go, and allow them to relax. See what happens. You may be pleasantly surprised to discover that you've learned to think the tension away.

Another way of learning relaxation is through auto-hypnosis, or *self-hypnosis*. Here is another relatively simple procedure. What it essentially involves is the ability to concentrate on something. We actually do this all the time without realizing it. Any time you are deeply absorbed in some activity, you are in a sense hypnotized. This can take the form of watching an interesting television show, reading a good book, or doing delicate needlework. Even a surgeon is absorbed while operating. During such activities, attention is so focused that other things may go unnoticed. An exciting episode on television, for instance, may prevent you from smelling the food that is burning on the stove. Like progressive muscle relaxation, learning to relax through self-hypnosis is a structured technique and needs persistence, consistency, and patience. Begin by selecting a quiet place to practice and make yourself comfortable in a chair. Take a deep breath and hold it for a while. As you begin to exhale, try to feel relaxation creeping into your entire body. Now select an object of concentration. This can be almost anything, like some spot on the wall. Keep your head straight, with your eyes tilted upward as they fixate on this object. Continue to get comfortable, and give yourself suggestions that you are relaxed and calm. Breathe slowly and regularly. After a while, you may notice that your eyelids are tired and that you want to close them. If so, go ahead and do this, while continuing to relax. Enjoy the relaxation until you are ready to end the procedure. If you do this for about ten minutes daily, you will be learning a very effective relaxation technique.

You can also learn to relax through light meditation. This strategy is related to hypnosis. Actually, the procedure outlined above is an example of light hypnosis. Both of these techniques can be "deepened," and go beyond relaxation, something that we'll examine later on. Meditation is like hypnosis, since it also deals with concentration. Benson[2] studied a variety of meditative procedures and found that they have four things in common. First is a quiet environment, and second is muscle relaxation. Third is an object of concentration, which can be a word, a sound, a chant, or almost anything. Fourth, and most important, is the need to adopt an effortless approach to the practice or what is called passive concentration. This may seem paradoxical at first, since we usually think of concentration as something that involves effort. Try to think of passive concentration as "effortless effort," as something that you allow to happen rather than force to happen. This is the kind of attitude that is essential to successful meditation. Using these four common elements, Benson developed a meditative procedure designed to produce the *relaxation response.* He derived this technique from transcendental meditation, a form a yoga. Unlike yoga, however, Benson's procedure is not presented within a spiritual context. The technique is simple to use, with the object of concentration being the number "one." Begin the practice by getting comfortably relaxed, and close your eyes. Now as you breathe in and out, say the number "one" to yourself every time you exhale. Continue doing this for about twenty minutes, all the while maintaining a passive attitude. If intrusive thoughts pop into your head, don't fight them, but gently ignore them and allow relaxation to take their place. If done over a period of time, this simple meditative technique will enable you to achieve a comfortable state of relaxation. Once again, persistence, consistency, and patience are vital for success.

As you can see, each of these procedures attempts to teach relaxation by focusing on something. This includes muscle reactions, as well as other internal or external stimuli. These approaches are not exhaustive, but represent some of the more popular trends in relaxation therapy. As we'll see later on, the Cayce readings often recommend relaxation as a therapeutic for a variety of psychological disorders. While learning to relax can be used as an end in itself, it is also often a preliminary step in the use of imagination as a coping skill. Let's turn to this next.

6

Using Your Imagination

. . . if there is the intense study of how *mind* is indeed the builder, [the entity] will see that what is held in the act of mental vision becomes a reality in the material experience.
Edgar Cayce reading 906-3

Then spiritualize and visualize purposes, in the manner in which the entity desires things to be done, and you'll have them done!
Edgar Cayce reading 3577-1

*The use of imagery in dealing with psychological prob*lems is found throughout the Cayce materials. This is to be expected in light of his basic tenet that creativity relates to the mind. Mind continually generates mental patterns. Once these become subconscious, they express themselves in automatic, habitual ways. Psychological disorders represent maladaptive habit patterns as they appear in the mind and body and in the individual's behavior. These habits can be overcome by the creation of new, more adaptive ones, and using imagination is one way of doing this.

We always use our imaginations. It occurs when we

daydream about the future, ruminate about the day's events, fantasize about something we'd like to have, and in many other ways. Most of the time imaginative processes are spontaneous. They originate from a variety of sources and are automatic in their expression. When they are maladaptive, they usually affect our behavior. For example, the claustrophobic who always fantasizes the dangers of being in an elevator avoids them at all costs. The use of imagination as a coping mechanism attempts to replace old mental habits with new ones. For the elevator phobic, this means switching her negative fantasies with more positive ones. Such changes in imagery generalize to real-life situations. This means that as the claustrophobic loses her fear of elevators when she visualizes them, she will also be unafraid as she uses them.

Imagery techniques can be used for all sorts of psychological problems. What they have in common is the attempt to focus attention on one's inner mental life in a predetermined, structured, and goal-oriented manner. In time, new mental habits are created. While this can be practiced in many ways, it is more effective when done in a relaxed state. Learning a relaxation technique, then, would be beneficial before beginning the use of imagery as a coping strategy. Another prerequisite is the preparation of a written or taped script to be used in learning the new mental habit patterns.

There are a variety of techniques that use imagery. One of them is *positive visualization*. Here, the psychological disorder is viewed in a new, constructive manner. Let's say that you're depressed about being overweight, and this is especially acute at social functions where you are more self-conscious. In using positive visualization to combat this, write out a sketch in which you portray yourself at a desired weight. You might picture yourself at a party where people are complimenting you. As

Fanning[1] tells us, try to use all of your senses in doing this. In addition to using visual imagery where you see yourself and others at the party, add elements like the sensation of the new clothes on your body, the sound of people talking to you, the aroma of the summer air, the taste of the soft drink you are sipping, and so on. The scenario becomes even more effective if you add detail to it. Here, you might picture the particulars of the music that is playing, or of what people are saying, etc. Movement also helps, as you see yourself dancing in a free and easy manner. It is also very important to incorporate all relevant emotions into your mental movie. Are you proud of yourself for losing weight? Do you feel exhilarated by the compliments you are receiving? Your scenario should focus on only the positives. Avoid scenes that have any negative connotations, such as feeling sad, eating fattening foods, and the like. You might also want to include a positive affirmation at the end of your sketch such as, "I love the way I look," or "I'm happy with myself." Take your time in writing everything out. It is important that you do this in your own words, since you have a unique style of imagery and an individual language that expresses it. Let your imagination go. Don't worry if your production is silly or foolish. After you write out your sketch, record it onto a tape. You are now ready to begin. Lie down, close your eyes, and relax as you listen to the tape. Try to get into it as you're doing this. If negative thoughts intrude, gently let them go. Be patient, and try to be consistent and persistent in your efforts. Practice your positive visualization at least once a day. Obviously, the more you do it, the better it will be for you.

Another imagery technique is *covert sensitization.* This is especially useful for those psychological disorders where a person finds pleasure in a habit which is not medically or socially very healthy. Included here would be a variety of sexual problems, issues revolving around anger, and addictive disorders like drinking and the use of drugs. Covert sensitization involves using imagery to connect the bad habit with painful consequences and a more positive one to pain relief. Once again, it is necessary to construct a vivid and detailed mental movie that you are going to "watch" in a relaxed state. Let's say that you are working with alcohol dependence. Write out a sketch where you see yourself drinking in some situation. Suppose it's a weekly gathering at a friend's house where you go to watch football on TV. Pick out your favorite chair and picture yourself holding a drink. Try to visualize the drink in all its aspects: what it looks like, how the glass feels in your hand, the aroma of the drink, and so on. Now bring the glass to your lips and begin drinking. Drink the entire glass. At this point, shift the scene abruptly and switch it to a very aversive situation. Imagine a sudden, unexpected gagging reaction, a feeling of nausea, and a need to vomit. Follow through by seeing yourself vomit on your friend's expensive rug. Picture this in as much detail as possible. See your recent meal come up, its smell, taste, etc. Also try to imagine the embarrassment and humiliation you feel. Now shift the picture again. See your friend taking you outside for a breath of fresh air, smell the air around you, and feel the distress dissipating. As your relish this relief, hear yourself saying that you'll never take another drink. This is the kind of sketch you would compose when using covert sensitization. Again, it should be put on tape and heard at least once a day, in a consistent manner. For the best results, be patient and persistent in your practice.

A somewhat different approach to using your imagination is seen in a technique known as *covert modeling*. This involves making believe that you are another person when you are confronted with your psychological problem. It has been found useful in treating many disorders where anxiety, depression, and other symptoms are present. The rationale for covert modeling is that if you successfully imagine another person doing something that is difficult for you, you can become like that person and overcome your dilemma. Let's see how this works by looking at non-assertiveness. People like this are usually very shy and self-conscious. They believe that their feelings don't count and that they have no right to express themselves, even if it is to say something positive. They usually find themselves agreeing with others. Non-assertiveness is a common symptom in people with social phobia, dependent personality disorder, and other psychological disorders.

Learning to be assertive through covert modeling begins by listing all the situations in your life in which you have trouble expressing yourself. These should be ranked from least, to most stressful. An example of a relatively nonstressful situation may be asking someone for the correct time, while a very stressful event may be disagreeing with an opinion. After you have constructed your list, think of a person whom you admire for his or her ability to be assertive. This can be almost anyone, from a close friend to someone you hardly know. Let this person serve as your role model. You are now ready to learn assertiveness in imagery. Sit in your favorite chair and get yourself very relaxed. Now try to visualize the least stressful encounter where you would behave in a non-assertive manner. Try to do this as vividly as possible, using both verbal and nonverbal imagery. At this point, bring your role model into the scene and merge yourself with this person. Make believe that you are behaving as he or she would. Focus on everything here, like language, facial expressions, eye contact, body language, and so on. Imagine yourself being very comfortable doing this. Visualize, also, a positive reaction from the person to whom you are asserting yourself. Following this, imagine additional rewards, like feeling good, getting a date, telling someone else about your success, and other such positive events. Identification with the role model as well as with positive consequences are both essential to success in covert modeling. Practice doing this in a consistent manner at least once a day. Begin with the least stressful situation. When you feel comfortable with it, proceed to the next item on your list. Continue in this manner until your have successfully completed all stressful situations. Again, patience and persistence are essential for success.

Imagery is also used in a procedure referred to as *imaginal desensitization.* This strategy was developed by Wolpe,[2] and has been found useful with problems involving fears, phobias, and interpersonal anxiety. It is based on the notion that fear can be overcome in stressful situations if one can learn to react in a manner that is incompatible with it. One such reaction is relaxation. Fear and relaxation do not mix. If you're feeling one of these, you cannot be feeling the other. So what you have to first learn in imaginal desensitization is a system of relaxation. Most often, progressive muscle relaxation is employed. Next you have to construct what is called an anxiety hierarchy. This is a list of the things that frighten you, arranged in order from least to most fearful. Suppose, for instance, that you are afraid of elevators. What part of this phobia is least frightening? If walking past an elevator scares you the least, make this number one in your hierarchy and write out a vivid scene of an actual elevator that produces this effect. Do the same for item number two, the next most frightening aspect. This might be standing in front of the elevator, seeing the elevator doors open, hearing the various sounds of the elevator, and so on. Continue in this manner until you have completed all aspects of the phobia. Put all the items of your hierarchy on tape. You are now ready to build your new habit pattern in imagery. Get yourself into a state of complete relaxation and listen to the first item on the list, the least frightening element. See yourself walking past the elevator and stay with this imagery for a few seconds. Now remove it from your mind and remain relaxed. Repeat this procedure again with the first item and continue in this manner until you can imagine the scene with no anxiety. At this point, move on to the second item of your hierarchy and do the same thing. Do this with all successive items until you have completely desensitized yourself to your fear. Again have patience, be persistent and consistent.

A final approach we'll consider in the use of imagination is not related to behavioral psychology but is seen in other models. It is also often recommended in the Cayce readings. This is the use of *suggestion*, which attempts to form a new mental pattern at the level of the subconscious mind. Perhaps the most popular approach here is hypnosis. We looked at light hypnosis earlier as a method of relaxation. Whenever you are relaxed, your consciousness is somewhere between an ordinary state and an altered state. The more relaxed you become, the more you approach the altered state and open the door, as it were, to your unconscious mind. It is here where you become more suggestible. This is what happens as hypnosis deepens and also when deep relaxation is incorporated with any strategy using the imagination. In other words, positive visualization, covert sensitization, covert modeling, and imaginal desensitization all become more effective, the more relaxed you are. In essence, then, these are all forms of hypnosis.

Although the readings recommend suggestive therapeutics, they don't always advise the services of a hypnotist in the treatment of psychological disorders. The reason for this is that the benefits of hypnosis relate to the personalities of both the hypnotist and the recipient of hypnotherapy. This means that if the intentions and goals of the hypnotist are misapplied in some way, the problem may not improve and may even worsen.

A more benign suggestive therapeutic recommended in the readings is *pre-sleep suggestion*. This makes use of a natural state of mind that we all experience, which psychologists call the hypnagogic state. It occurs when we go to bed at night. Often, we do not fall asleep immediately, but can identify a short period when we're not fully awake any more, yet not really asleep just yet. It's like an in-between state, where the outside world may appear in a distorted way, where thoughts may be less than rational, and where all sorts of feelings may pop up. It is during this time that the subconscious mind is very receptive to suggestion. As many people fall asleep mulling over their daily problems, what they are essentially doing is reinforcing negative subconscious habit patterns. Focusing on positive thoughts or affirmations during the hypnagogic state, then, is a relatively simple way of creating new mental patterns. Look at how one reading answered a question regarding a young child:

> Q. How can he be cured from the habit of sucking his thumb?
> A. This can be done by suggestion, if they will take the time to do so. As he goes to sleep, even though the thumb is in the mouth, take the time—take it from the mouth and suggest that the mind—suggest to the mind that he will not do same. Don't abuse him—don't discourage him save by the positive suggestion when he is going to sleep. 2289-6

Psychologists have found that pre-sleep suggestion can be used for many kinds of emotional problems (e.g., Budzynski)[3] and is relatively simple to employ. Begin by writing out a short scenario in which you picture yourself in a positive manner relative to the symptom you are working on. With depression and low self-esteem, for example, you might see yourself in a situation where you are smiling, laughing, and very happy. If this is difficult for you to do, you might instead, write out one or two short, positive affirmations, such as, "I am a good and caring person," or "I love myself just the way I am." Or you might even combine imagery with affirmation. In any event, after you write it out, put it on tape so that you can listen to it as you doze off to sleep. Remember that the hypnagogic state lasts for only a few minutes, so that whatever you're suggesting to yourself cannot be too long. It's better to have something that is short and repeated over and over. When you're ready to go to bed, start the tape at a low volume and listen to it as you fall asleep. Do this consistently for a few weeks. Remember too that you must be patient to get good results and be persistent in your efforts.

As you can see, there are many ways to use the power of imagination in working with psychological disorders. Most of these strategies are derived from behavioral psychology, and all of them are compatible with the recommendations made in the readings. We'll see this later when we examine specific emotional problems. Let's now turn our attention to another way of using the mind, this time through the power of reason.

7

Changing Your Thoughts

> . . . mind is the builder and that which we think upon may become crimes or miracles. For thoughts are things and as their currents run through the environs of an entity's experience these become barriers or stepping-stones, dependent upon the manner in which these are laid as it were.
>
> Edgar Cayce reading 906-3

Individuals with psychological disorders have char-acteristic thinking patterns. A hypochondriacal woman might dwell on some imagined terminal illness; a depressed man might think he's hopeless and helpless; and a paranoid individual might distrust others. Thoughts have a very interesting connection to feelings. One usually determines the other. If a woman really believed she were terminally ill, she would naturally be frightened. In the same manner, thoughts of hopelessness cause sadness, while those of deceit produce anger. To appreciate the link between thoughts and feelings, imagine walking down the street one day and seeing a friend of yours approaching. You greet her, but she walks right past you without saying anything. How would you feel? Well, this depends on how you interpret the situation. If you believe that she purposely snubbed you, you might feel angry; if you see it as rejection, you might feel sad; and, if you conclude that the event represents a first step in being excluded from an important social group, you might feel nervous. The important thing to see here is that the emotion relates to the way the situation is interpreted. It is not based on the actual event, but on what you said to yourself. If you see her the next day, a sense of relief would come over you if she greets you warmly and explains that she failed to see you earlier, as she was rushing to put money into a parking meter to avoid being ticketed.

Emotions of anger, sadness, and nervousness are most uncomfortable and are seen in a great number of psychological problems. These and other emotions take hold because individuals fail to question the validity of their underlying thought patterns. Such patterns are assumed to represent reality, but instead may be reflective of various *cognitive distortions,* or forms of destructive thinking. How would you know if your thoughts are like this? Burns[1] discusses ten different types of errors we make. See if any of these apply to you. One is called *all-or-none thinking*. This refers to looking at the world in black and white terms. People do this when they see themselves and others as "good vs. evil," "smart vs. dumb," "successful vs. failures," or other such extremes. Such thinking is destructive and can form the basis of emotional distress. For example, suppose you evaluate your school grades in terms of a "smart vs. dumb" dichotomy. If your grades are average, you may put yourself in the "dumb" category, which would contribute to a low self-esteem and depression.

Overgeneralization is the tendency to see one particular negative event as repeating itself in the future. If, for example, you fail to get a job offer following an interview, you would be overgeneralizing if you reasoned that you'll never get a job. People express this destructive pattern whenever they use words like "always" or "never." A woman who has a panic attack, and feels that she will always have such attacks, is overgeneralizing. Obviously, such thinking would contribute to her distress level and to the overall nature of her problem.

Another type of destructive thinking is called *mental filter.* Here, the person takes one negative event out of context and focuses on its significance. Suppose, for instance, that you have a party, and everybody seems to be having a good time except for one person who looks irritated. If you use a mental filter, you may think that the party is a failure because of this and get depressed.

Something similar occurs in *discounting the positive.* What happens here is that the person fails to give positive events the same weight as negative ones. If one person criticizes your work while another praises it, you would be expressing this destructive thinking pattern if you disregard the praise and focus only on the criticism. In psychological disorders this can be seen whenever a person has a good day emotionally but doesn't look at it in the same way as a bad one. The bad day is devastating relative to the overall problem, while the good one becomes insignificant.

Another cognitive distortion is *jumping to conclusions.* Here, a person formulates negative interpretations of events based on insufficient evidence. Conclusions are reached that are beyond question. One way this occurs is through *mind reading,* where motives and intentions are attributed to other people based on their behavior. A man comes home from work, for example, and notices that his wife is angry. Although the real reason for this is her frustration with the children, he "reads her mind" and relates it to a disagreement they had the evening before. As a result of his interpretation, he becomes defensive, and an argument begins. Mind reading is common in many psychological disorders. A hypochondriacal man may misinterpret the serious expression on the face of his physician as an indication that he is hiding something from him. A socially anxious woman may see the smile of an acquaintance as a polite gesture but believe that it betrays an underlying disapproval. In addition to mind reading, jumping to conclusions also occurs through *fortunetelling,* where people predict that bad things will happen to them. This can be seen in such statements as, "I'll probably get sick when I go on vacation next summer," or "I bet I don't get invited to the picnic." A man with a panic disorder expresses this destructive pattern when he predicts that his problem will lead to a nervous breakdown. A woman with a sexual dysfunction is thinking like this when she sees her marriage as ending due to her problem.

Magnification is another example of twisted thinking. This refers to a tendency to exaggerate events in life, to blow them out of proportion. Each event becomes a potential catastrophe, and the person spends endless time imagining the worst. This destructive pattern usually includes the words "what if" in one's thinking and always winds up with scenarios of doom and gloom. A student who is doing poorly in school would be catastrophizing as he thinks, "What if I fail this course? What if I don't graduate? What then? Suppose I don't get a job? What if I wind up on welfare?" Notice how magnification weaves a potentially devastating outcome. This distortion is common to many psychological problems. In the generalized anxiety disorder, for instance, a person always catastrophizes about life's events and appears unable to control it.

In *emotional reasoning* people see themselves as having permanent traits based solely on their feelings. For instance, sadness is an emotion and nothing more. If, however, a woman concludes that she must be a helpless person because of this feeling, she would be engaging in emotional reasoning. Another example would be a socially anxious man who reasons that he is interpersonally inept because of his fears.

Another cognitive error occurs whenever people evaluate their behavior against unrealistic standards. They make *should statements* and often use words like "I should" or "I must" in their thinking. What typically happens here is that the individual feels bad when things don't turn out as expected. A student, for example, who says he must get an A on an exam is devastated when he gets a B instead. Should statements are evident in all kinds of mental problems. Symptoms of anxiety and depression often include thoughts like "I should be interested" or "I should be successful" and many others.

In *labeling*, individuals attribute permanent traits to themselves and others based on transient expressions of behavior. This would occur, for instance, if you think of your neighbor as a chronic liar because she once lied to you, or if you see yourself as inherently stupid because of your inability to understand something in class. Labeling occurs in many emotional problems whenever people see themselves as intrinsically worthless, incompetent, inadequate, bad, and so on.

The last type of destructive thinking pattern is referred to as *personalization and blame*. Personalization occurs whenever a person assumes responsibility for everything that occurs in life. Suppose, for example, that you invite a friend to go fishing, and he catches a cold. You would be personalizing if you conclude that his cold was your fault. In psychological disorders, this type of thinking is often seen as patterns of inappropriate guilt. Such would be the case if a mother were to feel responsible for her son's poor school grades, even though she tried her best to help him. The opposite of personalization is blame. Here, you see others as responsible for every bad thing that happens in your life. If your fishing companion were to get more fish than you, he is to blame for your poor catch. This kind of reasoning is common in adolescents with oppositional defiant disorders who blame their parents, teachers, friends, and others for everything that goes wrong in their lives. It is also seen in alcoholics when they blame others for their drinking habits.

How reasonable is your thinking? Do any of these cognitive distortions apply to you? Sometimes two or more of them may be part of your thinking pattern, as there is considerable overlap between them. A depressed person, for instance, may conclude that, because he feels sad, he is an inherently inferior person (emotional reasoning); that people in life are generally happy or sad (all-or-none thinking); that his parents are to blame for his condition (blame); and that he will ultimately wind up in some kind of a mental institution (fortunetelling).

Destructive patterns in thinking can be challenged by a procedure of *thought restructuring.* This refers to a systematic use of reason to reorganize your thinking processes along more realistic lines and is a primary representative of the cognitive-behavioral approach. You begin first by looking at the thinking pattern as if it didn't belong to you, like it's something you're reading about. Now assume that you can win a big prize if you present evidence showing that the pattern was twisted in some way. You'd be surprised what you can come up with. Finally, based on this evidence, develop an alternative thinking pattern that is more realistic and constructive.

Let me show you some of the evidence that you can use to counter the cognitive distortions, beginning with all-or-none thinking. We saw that a person who thinks like this sees many things in life as falling into two categories. What's wrong with this kind of thinking? The answer is that it goes against the variability inherent in nature. As you examine the world around you, it becomes obvious that life cannot be lumped into two groups. Temperatures, for example, aren't just "hot" or "cold" but have many levels in between. If you feel cold when it's forty degrees outside, you don't feel hot when it rises to fifty. Instead, you feel less cold. The same holds true with human nature. An individual's school grades, for example, range from A to F, with many steps in between. This allows for many degrees of competence. One rational alternative, then, to dichotomous thinking is to think of traits as having gradations, rather than existing in two categories. A person with low self-esteem would feel less depressed if he interpreted his failure as a matter of degree, instead of in an either-or fashion.

Suppose the cognitive distortion is overgeneralization. What's the error in assuming that negative events repeat themselves? Again, the evidence in nature goes against it. Things are not always the same. "Never" is a very long time. A woman who has panic attacks and says that she will never be rid of them is thinking like this. Nothing happens this way in the world around us. As a rational alternative to overgeneralizing, try to eliminate words like "always" and "never" from your vocabulary and substitute them with words like "maybe" or "perhaps."

What is the challenge to mental filtering, where events are evaluated out of context? Again, look for the evidence after you objectify the distortion. Look at nature as a whole, with events occurring within this whole. A gray triangle appears one way alone and quite differently when viewed against a black or a white background. Taking things out of context alters both their meaning, as well as their significance. A woman with a body dysmorphic disorder, who is preoccupied and distressed by her facial wrinkles, is failing to look at her total situation in life. Doing so may change her entire outlook.

The error made in discounting the positive is that the individual fails to place equal value on positive and negative events. Positive events don't count. Again, the evidence is in nature, where all sorts of things happen from abundant food supplies to devastating earth changes. When we evaluate such events as good or bad, we are more objective and in agreement. This same kind of objectivity should be placed on events in our lives, with positive events given equal time with negative ones. So if you have a good day emotionally, try to make it count the way a bad one does.

How can you challenge the cognitive distortion of jumping to conclusions? With mind reading, where attributes and intentions are assumed, evidence is made possible as one considers alternative interpretations. The hypochondriacal man who is upset with his doctor's facial expression might entertain the thought that this has nothing to do with any medical condition but instead relates to a problem in the physician's personal life. Another challenge to mind reading is to check things out. The patient might just ask the doctor why he looks the way he does. Considering alternative hypotheses can also be employed in the fortunetelling error. If you tend to predict bleak future occurrences, tell yourself that other, more positive alternatives may occur. A woman with a sexual dysfunction might thus see her problem as a means of improving the communication with her husband, rather than the demise of her marriage.

How can you talk back to yourself when dealing with magnification, where you blow things out of proportion? You have an anxiety disorder and worry unrealistically about the potential loss of your job. In looking for evidence, the first thing you might do is to figure the odds of this happening. If you catastrophize, you tend to think in a "what if" fashion, so the odds have to be calculated in a step-by-step manner. Thoughts like "What if the economy gets bad?" followed by "What if my industry is affected?" followed by "What if my department is affected?" followed by "What if my job rating is poor?" followed by "What if I get laid off?" are all examples of steps in the evaluation of probabilities. Such an exercise in itself may prove quite helpful, as individuals often see a decline in odds when doing this. It is important that your odds are realistic. A claustrophobic planning a vacation to Las Vegas may give herself realistic odds regarding the outcome of her gambling spree but very unrealistic ones regarding a potential plane crash. Another form of evidence for magnification is to compare your present thinking to similar patterns in the past. Did your previous worries materialize? If not, use this as evidence against your present ones.

In emotional reasoning, individuals infer personality traits based on the way they feel. The evidence against this is to understand that feelings fluctuate and change. If personality traits were based on feelings, then they would be as variable as the feelings themselves. As we have seen, however, personality traits are unique, and this is what you should focus on in dealing with emotional reasoning. If, for example, you get nervous at social gatherings, this does not mean that you are interpersonally inferior. Ask yourself how you act when you are at a family function. Isn't it true that you are more comfortable here? Can you then reasonably conclude that you are inferior in a social situation? The answer is obvious, as you come to see that emotions can be quite deceiving.

Should statements are errors in thinking where we evaluate actions against some standard. The mistake here is in viewing these standards as rigid and absolute.

A person with a messy apartment may feel guilty if he believes that it should be neat, even though his apartment is a reflection of himself. The reason for his guilt is that he is evaluating his behavior against the standard of other people, and he never bothers to question them. One way to challenge this form of thinking is to examine the basis of your standards. In many cases, they reflect the views of your parents and family. If this is the case, evaluate whether or not they are appropriate for you. If they are not, determine what your own, inherent standards are and make a concerted effort to follow them. Standards are relative. What constitutes a preferred form of behavior for others may not relate to you.

The destructive thinking pattern seen in labeling is the tendency to confuse people with their behavior. The evidence against doing this is to recognize that individuals are complex and, as such, do many different things in life. Behavior, however, doesn't constitute one's inner self. A person's inability to fix a flat tire, for example, doesn't warrant the personality trait of incompetence, any more than his digesting food makes him a digester! The mistake of labeling is often seen in the view people take when they have emotional problems. Instead of viewing their symptomatic behavior as one out of many other behaviors, they use it to stigmatize themselves as mentally ill.

Finally, there is the thinking distortion of personalization and blame, where the error involves a misunderstanding of control and a misattribution of responsibility. The evidence against this is the recognition that human beings have free will and are responsible for their own behavior. A woman who feels guilty for her son's poor academic performance would challenge her thinking pattern here by attributing some degree of responsibility to her son for his grades. The same holds true when others are always blamed for one's misfortunes. The defiant adolescent would question his own contribution to events in his life, and the alcoholic would not blame her husband's neglect for her drinking.

As you can see, thought restructuring involves the use of reason to challenge destructive thinking patterns. Looking for evidence against the distortion is a good way to do this. The bottom line here is to see that your thinking does not agree with the realities of your natural and social worlds. Also beneficial is the attempt to make the distortion objective, to assume that it does not relate to you.

To use thought restructuring as a self-help strategy, begin by identifying your cognitive distortion and writing it down. This helps to objectify it, as well as providing the necessary help to accomplish your goals. Now, look for all the evidence you can to counter it and write this down as well. After you've done this, write out an alternative thinking pattern that is more constructive and try to see how it makes sense to you. You can also reinforce your reasoning efforts by trying to overtly express this new pattern. You can read it into a tape recorder, recite it in front of a mirror, tell somebody else about it, or even sing it for that matter. Any of these activities can help in establishing your new mental habit. As this becomes consolidated, you'll feel better, because as your thinking changes in a more constructive direction, so too does your emotion. As with all self-help strategies, persistence is important. Since old mental habits are fairly well established, you'll have to be patient in your attempt to change them.

Cognitive distortions are usually based on more general, enduring *irrational beliefs.* Like cognitive distortions, these are learned from a variety of sources, including parents, friends, teachers, books, the mass media, and others. Ellis[2] identifies twelve such beliefs and feels that they are the root causes for many psychological difficulties. His reasoning is similar to what we said earlier: namely, that what we think determines how we feel. If our thinking is based on irrational patterns, then our feelings will follow suit.

As you consider the following irrational beliefs, try to see how they relate to the cognitive distortions we just examined. If you can identify with any of them, look at its rational alternative and see if you can figure out why it makes more sense. If you cannot, try to work with evidence against the irrational belief, as you would with cognitive distortions, until the reason comes to you.

Irrational Belief: I must be loved by everyone for everything I do.
Rational Belief: I should love and respect myself, and focus on loving others.

Irrational Belief: Certain things that people do are evil, and they ought to be punished.
Rational Belief: Certain things that people do are inappropriate, and they are done out of ignorance, stupidity, or psychological disturbance.

Irrational Belief: It is just awful when things don't go the way I'd like them to go.
Rational Belief: It's unfortunate if things aren't going my way, and I should try to change them, but if I cannot, I should accept them as they are.

Irrational Belief: Psychological problems are caused by external events.
Rational Belief: Psychological problems are caused by the interpretations one makes of external events.

Irrational Belief: I should be very concerned about frightening things in my life.

Rational Belief: I ought to deal with frightening things or if I cannot, stop dwelling on how terrible they are and attempt to think of other things.

Irrational Belief: I should avoid problems in life. This is the easier path for me to take.
Rational Belief: Problems should be faced as they occur. Avoiding them only produces future complications.

Irrational Belief: I need something stronger than myself to rely on.
Rational Belief: I should have faith in myself and in my abilities.

Irrational Belief: I should be competent in everything I do.
Rational Belief: As a human being, I am fallible and limited in my capabilities.

Irrational Belief: Bad things that happened to me in the past must affect me forever.
Rational Belief: I should learn from my experiences but not let them affect my present behavior.

Irrational Belief: Other people should do things as I see them.
Rational Belief: Other people have their own problems, and the worst way to help them is to have them see things my way.

Irrational Belief: People are happiest when they are inactive.
Rational Belief: People are happiest when they pursue creative ends or are focused on others.

Irrational Belief: I have no control over my feelings.

Rational Belief: I can control my feelings by keeping my thought patterns rational.

As you can see, irrational beliefs, like cognitive distortions, are forms of destructive thinking. They represent more fundamental, elementary patterns and often provide the basis for the formation of the cognitive distortion. The method of changing them, however, remains that of thought restructuring. Again, this involves objectifying the irrational belief by writing it down and also indicating all the arguments against it, as well as those in support of its rational alternative. Using your power of reason, the new belief is gradually assimilated as a new mental habit pattern. It is also beneficial to express this belief in some overt manner, as this will help to consolidate the process. Be patient and persistent, and in time you will see positive change.

8

Modifying Your Behavior

It is not the knowledge, then, but what one does with one's
abilities, one's opportunities in relationships to others, that
makes for the development or retardment of that individual.
Edgar Cayce reading 1293-1

The above coping strategies encompass some of the more
popular ways of dealing with psychological disorders by
working with the mind itself. Whether you use techniques
of imagination or reasoning skills, you are attempting to
form new mental habits in place of old ones. The strategies that we will now look at use a different approach in
the formation of habits. They assume that since habits
involve some sort of action, they can be addressed at the
level of behavior. Forming new habit patterns thus means
forming new behaviors. These, in turn, will automatically alter any associated underlying mental patterns.

Psychological problems are often expressed at the

level of behavior. A man complains, for example, that he eats too much because of his depression. A claustrophobic woman avoids elevators. A man with an obsessive-compulsive disorder is consumed with cleaning rituals. A pedophile sexually molests little children. A hypochondriac is always going to the doctor. The alcoholic cannot stop drinking.

Behaviors occur in certain situations and are usually followed by some consequences. *Operant strategies* attempt to produce changes in behavior by altering this sequence in some way. They ask you to look at what you do, where you do it, and what happens right after you do it. Some operant strategies focus on the consequences of behavior. What is the effect of overeating on the depressed man? How does the claustrophobic woman feel after she decides not to get on the elevator? What is the payoff for the individual with the cleaning compulsion, the pedophile, and the hypochondriac? How does the alcoholic feel after he drinks?

Consequences of behavior can be put into two categories. One of these is *rewards*. Rewards are usually things that make you feel good. Other consequences are *punishments,* or things that make you feel bad. Both rewards and punishments affect the behavior that precedes them. If you feel good after you do something, you'll probably do it again. If you feel bad, however, this will lessen your future behavior. The woman who avoids elevators, for example, feels relief, and this in turn serves as a reward which continues her behavior pattern. The man who compulsively cleans finds comfort in the conviction that his behavior will prevent some catastrophe.

Some operant strategies attempt to change maladaptive habit patterns by manipulating rewards and punishments. One of them works with rewards and is called *positive reinforcement.* Its premise is simple. It says that if behavior is followed by positive effects, it will be maintained or stay with you. A positive reinforcement can be a simple thing, like a cup of coffee. It can also be something more extravagant, like going on a vacation. It can even be something that you say to yourself, like, "I did a good job!" Positive reinforcement can be used as a self-help technique for a variety of psychological disorders. It is especially helpful for those problems which show a deficit in behavior. Suppose, for instance, that you are non-assertive, and this contributes to a low self-esteem. The first thing you have to do is to define the behavior that you would like to work on. It would be best to begin with something simple, like learning to ask for the correct time of day. Here, you might approach three strangers each day and ask them what time is it. On each occasion, reward yourself in some way. Pick something that you can apply after the desired behavior occurs, like a candy bar, a self-statement, like, "I did it," or anything else that can be easily employed. What is important here is that you reinforce yourself immediately after the new assertive behavior occurs. If you wait too long, the reward will lose its effectiveness. As you find yourself having less and less difficulty in this task, add another level to it, like asking somebody for directions. Follow the same procedure of making positive reinforcement contingent with this behavior until it, too, becomes a new habit. Continue in this manner until you have reached your desired goal of assertiveness. Keep notes on what you're doing, as this will provide organization to the procedure. Include here items like time, day, place, and anything else that you feel may be relevant.

A second operant approach involves the use of *aversion techniques*. These strategies are behavioral variations of covert sensitization, which we examined earlier as an imagery technique. They make use of aversive, or punishing stimuli, in order to reduce undesirable behaviors. Such behaviors reflect things that people do for their immediate positive effects, but which are detrimental in the long run. Problems such as compulsive disorders, alcohol and drug dependence, sexual deviations, and overeating would be included here. The basis of aversion strategies is that if the behavior becomes associated with negative consequences, it will diminish. There are many ways of doing this. Let's suppose that you want to stop smoking. You smoke a pack of cigarettes daily and decide to make as your goal a half a pack a day for a period of one week. Write this down, as well as what the punishment will be if you exceed this level. The aversive stimulus should be practical to administer, and applied immediately following the occurrence of the undesirable behavior. If you smoke more than you intend, for instance, you might call up somebody you dislike, engage in some undesirable housework, refrain from watching your favorite TV show, or anything else that is disagreeable to you. If you succeed in your efforts, modify the procedure with a new goal of smoking only five cigarettes daily for the next week. Continue in this manner until you have reached your desired level of attainment.

There are many different ways in which aversion techniques can be employed. For example, in a *satiation* approach, the individual engages in the behavior until its undesirable components outweigh its desirable ones. With cigarette smoking, this means that the person would continuously smoke one cigarette after another, until he felt sick. As a result, smoking would become distasteful. Satiation should not be considered for every such problem, however; obviously, it would not work for habits such as alcohol dependence.

Aversion techniques work best when they are used in conjunction with positive reinforcement. This means that rewards should be applied when the undesirable behavior is avoided in the same way that punishments are given when it is not. For example, the smoker who meets his daily goal of cigarettes might reward himself in some way, just as he punishes himself when he fails to do so. There are many ways of combining rewards and punishments. They only require your imagination. Don't forget to write out your procedure in detail to get the most beneficial effects.

Working with rewards and punishment is not the only manner of effecting changes in behavior. Another thing you can do is to change the situation in which the behavior occurs. As stated earlier, activities occur in specific situations. These can include anything, like being in your kitchen, watching TV, reading a book, etc. One way of dealing with maladaptive patterns, then, is to change these situations. This is the basis of an operant strategy known as *stimulus control*. Let's examine this more closely by looking first at aspects of the physical environment. If you were to observe your behavior on any given day, you would notice that many of the things that you do are automatic reactions to your location. When you walk into an elevator, for example, the first thing you do after pressing the appropriate button is to turn around and face the door. You do this regardless of where these buttons are and whether or not there are other people in the elevator with you. Your behavior is under the control of the elevator, which serves as the immediate stimulus. In a similar way, other aspects of your physical environment produce consistent reactions: an opera brings you to tears; a shopping mall makes you spend money; a hot dog stand excites your hunger drive; a funeral makes you somber and pensive; and reading inspirational literature makes you think about life. In the same manner, your social environment makes you react in certain ways. When you are with friends you may be carefree and relaxed. At social functions, where you meet new people, you may feel more up-tight and self-conscious. Other examples would include your home, job, leisure activities, etc.

The essence of stimulus control is to change some aspect of your environment so that different, more desirable behaviors can occur. This technique can be used for many psychological problems including overeating, non-assertiveness, smoking, sexual problems, insomnia, and others. How do you do it? Let's say that you're overweight. You begin by examining all the situations that relate in some way to food, like where you eat, whom you eat with, what magazines and books you read about food, where you shop, and so on. To effect stimulus control, alter these situations in some manner. For example, arrange to eat in only the kitchen and dining areas at home and to eliminate eating in other rooms. In time, any cues associated with eating in these areas will be eliminated. In addition, you might keep only low-calorie food at home or enough food for a short period of time. Or, you might decide to bring your behavior under the control of a clock by eating at only predetermined times. You might do your food shopping only after you've eaten, to prevent overeating due to hunger pangs. Or better yet, you might take a shopping list with you and buy only what's on the list. Use your imagination to create a new environment for yourself. If you are satisfied with the results, modify the strategy with additional controls. Take a new route home from work to avoid the temptation of the pizzeria. Arrange to eat at restaurants which specialize in low-calorie foods or eat only with friends who are weight conscious. Read books about successful dieters. There are many possibilities here. Once again, write down everything you intend to do.

Stimulus control methods vary in complexity. Sometimes they are relatively simple, involving only small environmental changes. This would be the case with *bibliotherapy*, where you incorporate reading materials into your self-help program. You could read certain things, or avoid some types of material. Reading often puts us in certain moods and instigates mood-congruent behavior patterns. At other times, stimulus control methods can be quite dramatic, as when a person is admitted to a psychiatric facility for treatment. The mental institution is also an example of this procedure and a radical one at that. You can use stimulus control as your sole strategy, or it can be combined with any other technique. The overeater, for instance, can probably benefit more by combining it with techniques like positive visualization, covert modeling, or other strategies in challenging the problem.

In addition to the use of operant strategies in dealing with psychological disorders, there are other approaches derived from respondent conditioning. One of these is *in vivo desensitization*. This is actually a real-life application of imaginal desensitization, the technique described earlier. Here, if you recall, the goal was to learn to associate relaxation responses to imagined feared situations arranged in a hierarchy from least to most threatening. In real-life desensitization, you attempt to do the same thing but in actual situations, instead of in imagery. You learn to associate the feared object with security, rather than anxiety. Once again, this technique can be quite effective for a variety of problems, especially those which have a fear component. Let's look at it, using the same example of the elevator phobic described earlier. The first thing to do here is to construct an anxiety hierarchy. List all the aspects of the phobia and arrange them in order, from least troublesome to most nerve racking. Let's say that the least frightening element for you is walking past the elevator. You become more nervous as you stand in front of the elevator, see the doors open and close, hear its many sounds, enter the elevator, etc. Rank all these components of your phobia. You are now ready to begin desensitization proper.

This requires your *exposure* to the feared situations in a step-by-step manner. For example, you might spend a predetermined amount of time each day walking past an elevator. You would do this every day until all discomfort and anxiety have dissipated. After mastering the first item on the hierarchy, proceed to the next one and repeat the procedure. Continue in this manner until you achieve your goal and your phobia is completely gone. In addition to writing out your anxiety hierarchy, also indicate the specifics of what you'll be doing, including things like location, time, objects, and anything else that's relevant.

As you can see, there are many ways to form new habit patterns by working with your behavior. Each of these techniques can be used in isolation or in combination with each other. Moreover, behavioral strategies can be combined with those using relaxation, imagination, and reason. At times, this may be a recommended approach. For example, in working with real-life desensitization, you may do better if you first learn to desensitize your fears in imagery and then gradually lead into a real-life situation. Regardless of how you use these procedures, patience is needed in all of them. Old habits are fairly well established, and they cannot be easily replaced. It is for this reason that persistence is also necessary. Whatever you choose to do, it needs to be practiced repeatedly. The more you do it, the better the results. Finally, make an attempt to be consistent if the technique calls for it. Try to do the same thing, in the same place, at the same time, and in the same way. Doing this makes the habit simple and unitary, as opposed to one that is complex, which would occur if the procedure is varied. As simple habit patterns form more quickly than complex ones, consistency in practice helps you to reach your goals more quickly.

9

Working with Spiritual Ideals

First, know thy ideals—physical, mental and spiritual. And know the physical result is first conceived in spirit, acted upon by mind, and then manifested in the material—with what spirit ye entertain.   Edgar Cayce reading 2813-1

The self-help techniques that we considered are all based on the rationale that psychological symptoms represent maladaptive habits and that symptom relief occurs as new habit patterns are formed. This can occur by learning to relax, by using your imagination and reasoning skills, or by working directly with your behavior. The Cayce readings concur with this idea, as they too see the habitual nature of psychological disorders and they stress a need to form new habits as a way of correcting old ones. However, as we have seen, the readings view a habit pattern as the offshoot of events related to other dimensions of reality. These events revolve around a Big

I which constantly seeks to express itself. The manner of this expression, from its inception as a soul, defines the entity. In this paradigm, psychological disorders reflect imbalances created by the Big I in its journey through various spiritual dimensions or mind. These imbalances can also be viewed as a conflict between personality and individuality. The little I of personality is its self-awareness. It is guided by selfish interests and seeks to express its separateness. The Big I of individuality, however, seeks to express its nature as part-within-a-whole, and herein lies the war.

The psychological problem then is multifaceted and has spiritual, mental, and physical determinants. Spiritual factors interface with the body's endocrine system, while mental factors interface with the autonomic nervous system. As spirit, mind, and body are interdependent and interact with each other, the treatment approach of the readings is holistic. It addresses a system in conflict and assumes that little can be accomplished otherwise. Attempts to work with habits at the level of immediate causation may prove fruitless, as they always relate to more remote factors within the system. Although symptom relief can occur by dealing with immediate causes, the cure may be temporary. This was evident in certain readings where the sleeping Cayce asked why the individuals were seeking help. If they wanted freedom from suffering and a return to their normal lifestyles, the readings indicated that it was these very styles that produced their problems in the first place. This idea can be likened to someone who goes on a crash diet, only to return to former eating patterns once the goal is accomplished and regain the weight.

To understand this better from the larger perspective of remote causes, return for a moment to the example we used earlier of the hydrophobic individual. Suppose that his near-drowning experience in childhood represented the effects of a previous life where he drowned someone. If this is his karma, what should he do about it? According to the readings, the best course of action is to see the problem as a spiritual correction and to treat it within this context. His treatment strategy should view the problem as an opportunity for spiritual growth and focus on this as his goal. For instance, in seeking a cure, he might look at the ability it will provide to help children who have handicaps similar to his, or to enjoy the beauties of nature more, or other such higher goals. He might work with any of the techniques we discussed. He could use imaginal desensitization and visualize the components of his fear in a graduated fashion, or do the same thing with real-life exposure. He could employ positive visualization and learn to associate swimming with the rewards inherent in his higher goals. He could make use of thought restructuring to correct cognitive distortions and irrational beliefs. The bottom line in his self-help efforts is to work with his phobia within the context of his individuality, not his personality.

If his curative efforts revolved around personality, he might be seeking symptom relief as an escape from the humiliation and embarrassment associated with his phobia, or as a means of acquiring a skill needed to compete in swim meets, or other ego-related goals. Again, he could use any psychological strategy to accomplish these ends and get positive effects. By not addressing the basic issue, however, the phobia may return at some future point in his life or in a subsequent lifetime.

In addition, by focusing on immediate causes, he may be creating new karmic patterns. If, for example, he overcomes his phobia by working with the reward value of swimming competitions, he may overcompensate his personality in this direction. He may frequently enter such competitions and boast about his accomplishments at the expense of others. As he enhances his personality like this, he is setting up a new trend which will eventually be corrected. This itself can take a variety of forms. Hypothetically, he may be reborn into a future lifetime where his competitive efforts always meet with failure, due to some emotional or physical handicap. He can even have this new problem in addition to the recurrence of his hydrophobia!

In addressing remote as well as immediate causes, the readings at once provide symptom relief while avoiding these problems. The psychological disorder is addressed as a systemic conflict, and the treatment attempts to replace "bad" habits of personality with "good" ones of individuality. In doing so, the readings evaluate the person, not the person's psychological problem. They see symptom relief as a natural accompaniment to the transformation of personality which accompanies spiritual actualization. As such, there is a permanent solution to the problem.

All causes of suffering lie in the realm of patterns which exist in every spiritual dimension or on every level of mind. In ordinary reality, these patterns translate as habits when one suffers from a psychological disorder. Both immediate and remote causes result from poor choices misaligning a pattern from its divine framework and initiating corrective measures. These choices could have been made by the present "I" that you identify with or by earlier "I's." Even the Big I of the soul made choices that missed the mark from the moment of its inception.

The transformation of personality involves the experience of one's true nature as a Big I, as well as the ideal expression of this I in its journey through mind. In other words, you have to experience yourself as a creator and see your ideal creation as that which it is, an expression of the real you. You are not that which you have created, regardless on which level of mind it exists. It is here, in the realm of patterns, that psychological disorders have their origins.

How can you do this? How can you transform your personality and bring psychological problems to a permanent end? The readings tell us that it is first necessary to assume that the problem reflects the operation of patterns in conflict. Second, they invite you to attempt to identify your perfect pattern, or the ideal expression of your Big I, and to harmonize with it. Working with the pattern in this manner increases your mobility, or degrees of freedom. Why should this be so?

Perhaps an analogy will help here. Make believe that you are an astronaut on a mission to the moon. As you are landing, your spacecraft malfunctions, and you crash. The result of the accident is amnesia, and you have no idea who you are, where you are, or where you came from. The only thing left from the crash is a large mirror in which you see a reflection of yourself in your spacesuit. This reflection is what you think you are. In a short time, you begin to feel uncomfortable, as the spacesuit needs to be adjusted for oxygen, but you have no idea how to do this. You try various maneuvers and in time figure it out. Other problems soon follow, and you solve these as well. You eventually learn all the operations of the spacesuit and, in so doing, diminish your suffering.

This same idea applies in working with the ideal expression of your Big I. Your psychological problems reflect the operation of laws related to patterns. Like the astronaut stuck on the moon, you are stuck in a habit pattern. The transformation of personality requires learning the operation of these laws and a willingness to harmonize with them. Since you are not in tune with your Big I, however, you have to begin with your little I, which is the only link you have with it. This means that you have to work with self-awareness and with your personality traits as they revolve around it in order to find your true nature.

The readings suggest that you begin this quest by first defining your *spiritual ideal*. This reflects the highest notion that you hold about spiritual reality. Spiritual ideals come to mind as we examine the meaning of life and death, the nature of God, where we came from, where we are going, and other existential questions. One reading defines it like this:

> . . . thy spiritual concept of the ideal, whether it be Jesus, Buddha, mind, material, God or whatever is the word which indicates to self the ideals spiritual. 5091-3

Notice that the "word" can refer to non-spiritual things like "material" or "mind." These are often the ideals of individuals who do not adhere to spiritual realities. For them, the bigger picture of things may be nothing more than what they experience in life, and their ideals revolve around ordinary, everyday events. The readings say that to do this is to confuse "ideas" with "ideals." Spiritual ideals assume a spiritual reality. As they are ineffable, however, they can be expressed only through our ideas. One reading puts this in quite a lovely way:

> They are *not* of the earth, though they may manifest in same. For ye see them in the face of nature, in the beauty of a rose, in the smile of a baby. 262-98

This doesn't mean that a person who doesn't believe in spiritual realities cannot expect a transformation in personality. For each person exists at his or her specific level of development. Each is given the opportunity to find the Big I. If temporal goals like money, success, social aspirations, and others define one's ideals, they can be advantageous if they are in harmony with the divine pattern. This pattern emanates from God. Its source is infinite love, and it reflects creativity and oneness. Spiritual ideals revolve around these concepts. In our world of ordinary reality, such concepts are not comprehended directly. Instead, we experience their shadows, which appear as aspects of our personalities. These include traits like love, patience, mercy, long-suffering, kindness, gentleness, and others. Spiritual ideals can begin with any one of these traits, and incorporate others as we approach the divine pattern. Personality is transformed into individuality once the Big I expresses its true nature, in harmony with this pattern. Since all souls emanate from God, the ideal expression of each is a variation of this pattern.

A spiritual ideal is a standard of reference for daily living. It has to be a guidepost for everything one does in life. In this respect, it is very different from an ordinary goal. A goal is limited to specific, everyday concerns of personality. This includes things like losing weight, earning a good test grade, getting a job promotion, and things of this sort. In contrast, a spiritual ideal is an affirmation of the spiritual basis of one's existence. It is pervasive and consumes all areas of life. It is a daily point of reference.

The spiritual ideal differs from an ordinary goal in yet another way. This has to do with how one measures progress. Progress toward goals is evaluated within the context of personality. For instance, if a person wants to lose weight, he diets and exercises and uses the bathroom scale to see how well he's doing. A spiritual ideal, however, cannot be measured like this. We cannot get the kind of feedback that we're use to getting with goals. How, then, is progress measured? The answer is in a slow, gradual change in consciousness, where things are seen from a different line of reasoning. Ordinary consciousness is expanded and incorporates new modes of experience.

This relates to still another way in which goals differ from spiritual ideals. Goals are ephemeral, and as such, they are attainable. Spiritual ideals are not. That is to say, they are not attainable within the confines of ordinary consciousness. They are constantly in flux and represent an ongoing process of spiritual becoming. Progress in this direction reflects not only shifts in consciousness but variations in the nature of the ideal. Actualization results in the manifestation of individuality, with the full expression of one's true nature.

Let's go back to the analogy of the violin player to help understand this better. Remember how his favorite tune symbolized his personality, while the score for violin expressed his individuality? Remember also how he had certain potential choices? He could continue playing his own melody or get more involved with the score. Let's suppose he decides to work with the score and attempts to modify his melody to harmonize with the symphony. In composing the score, he refers to certain standards of musical arrangement along the way. These standards change as he gets closer to completion, but they all revolve around the basic theme of the symphony. Like musical standards, spiritual ideals change as one undergoes personality transformation, even though all ideals reflect the one divine pattern.

In working with spiritual ideals, the readings highlight a model to use as the perfect example. This is the Christ. While the Cayce material incorporates many diverse spiritual, theological, and philosophical views, the life and work of Jesus lie at the pinnacle of its approach. The rationale for this is beyond the scope of this book, and the interested reader can refer to a variety of sources for further elucidation of this (e.g., Drummond).[1] Suffice it to say that Edgar Cayce, himself a devout Christian, had to considerably restructure his own religious thinking to assimilate the very dissonant information he was getting from his readings. The bottom line is that the perfect pattern is inherent in the Christ. Because the essence of this pattern lies in the fatherhood of God and the fellowship of humanity, it coincides with the beliefs of many people, from many different traditions. Spiritual ideals that follow this pattern are the most efficacious ones to work with.

How can you identify your spiritual ideal? This is not an easy question to answer. One way to do this is to seriously look at some of the existential issues mentioned above. In doing so, look at what rings true for you. A spiritual ideal should not be something that another person tells you about or something you read in a book. You ought to personally identify with it. Thurston[2] points this out, as well as defines five universal characteristics shared by ideals. These are:

1. An expansion of consciousness—a sense of wonder. An ideal should increase your ordinary state of consciousness to incorporate other levels of reality. This, in turn, will enhance your wonder about life.

2. Service to others. A spiritual ideal is based on the transpersonal nature of being and embraces an altruistic quest.

3. Closeness to God. A spiritual ideal will bring you closer to a personal experience of God.

4. A view of purposefulness in all of life. In engendering a transpersonal view of reality, a spiritual ideal enables you to see the actualization directive in all areas of life.

5. Joy in life. The choice of the correct spiritual ideal will eventually bring you an element of happiness unsurpassed in your life.

Let's see how this works by looking at ideals in relationship to different psychological disorders. At one extreme, a chosen ideal may be diametrically opposed to the problem. For instance, a person who is depressed sees love as the center of spiritual reality, while he holds on to feelings of self-condemnation. At the other extreme, the psychological problem may represent a distorted version of the spiritual ideal. Such would be the case with the individual who sees order and harmony in the universe and expresses this through her obsessive-compulsive personality disorder, where she is preoccupied with details and rules, organization, and perfectionism. In choosing a spiritual ideal, see how it relates to your psychological disorder. You might, for example, express higher traits that are unrelated to your problem. You might, on the other hand, reframe the nature of your problem and coordinate your ideal to this. You might even combine these approaches. Once your spiritual ideal is determined, the next thing you have to do is to establish new habit patterns that are based on it. There are two steps in doing this. The first one involves translating the spiritual ideal into a *mental ideal*. The readings define this as:

> . . . the ideal mental attitude, as may arise from concepts of the spiritual, in relationship to self, to home, to friends, to neighbors, to thy enemies, to things, to conditions. 5091-3

The mental ideal, then, refers to the formation of new attitude patterns enabling you to work with your spiritual ideal in a way that's real for you. The word *attitude*, as used here, refers to the way you perceive, think, and feel about all aspects of your life, from "relationships" to "conditions." Old attitude patterns are to be replaced by new ones that use the spiritual ideal as a standard of reference. The next step is to translate the mental ideal into daily action. As the mental ideal reflects new attitudes to be learned, the *physical ideal* represents new behavior patterns. The readings define these as being:

> Not of conditions but what has brought, what does bring into manifestation the spiritual and mental ideals. What relationships does such bring to things, to individuals, to situations? 5091-3

The physical ideal relates to the way you express your spiritual and mental ideals day by day. With the spiritual ideal as a guidepost for the formation of new attitudes, how are these brought "into manifestation" in various situations, with different people, etc.? To illustrate the relationship between ideals, consider a hypothetical case of a person with a paranoid personality disorder. This individual basically doesn't trust others. He feels that people use him and is threatened by them. He cannot confide in others, holds grudges, and is very unforgiving. In working with ideals, he begins by examining his religious beliefs. Here, he sees that one of the basic attributes he gives to God is forgiveness. He decides to set this as his spiritual ideal and attempts to see how he can assimilate it into his personality. He asks himself, "What would be my ideal relationship to others, if I forgave them the way I feel that God forgives me?" He answers this by defining a certain attitude where he would not bear grudges and would be forgiving of insults and slights. He decides to make this attitude his mental ideal. He also considers how he would act toward others if he held such an attitude. He sees that he would be friendly to people even when they wrong him in some way. He makes this behavior pattern his physical ideal. Once ideals are defined, the next step is to begin working with them. This means changing your daily attitudes and behaviors in the direction of the ideals you've chosen. To do this, make use of the various psychological strategies discussed earlier and begin with simple things. You might, for example, pick one target person to work with. The paranoid individual can decide to do this with a neighbor against whom he has been holding a grudge for a long time. He can examine his thought pattern and look for possible twists in his thinking that contribute to his unforgiving attitude. He can see how he labels others and recognize the absurdity of doing this as he realizes that human beings, including his neighbor, are really miniature versions of God. He can work with his imagination by using covert modeling. Here, he would create a mental movie in which he pictures someone who is very forgiving behaving in a certain way and slowly merges himself with this person. Or he can make use of pre-sleep suggestions and focus on affirmations related to forgiveness. He can also work more directly with his behavior. He can make a friendly overture to his neighbor and reward himself with a pat on the back. Or he can use stimulus control and place himself in those situations where the atmosphere is one of forgiveness. These could include reading inspirational materials, surrounding himself with people who are forgiving by nature, and many other possibilities.

Working with ideals takes time. As we have seen, once a spiritual ideal is set, it has to be spelled out and applied in psychological and behavioral terms. These should be defined within the context of your personality and relate to your psychological problem. It is best to start out with something simple to work on. Again, everything you attempt to do should be written down for the best possible results. The readings recommend that ideals be arranged in three columns, representing the spiritual, mental, and physical, respectively. Whether you use this approach or any others, writing is important, as are patience and persistence.

In using ideals to solve your psychological problems,

you are on the road to symptom relief, as well as personality transformation. This occurs with the fuller manifestation of your individuality, as the Big I expresses its
ideal self more and more. This practice also facilitates
attunement with this Big I as creator, and with its patterns as creations.

Let's return to the moon analogy to see what this
means. Recall that the astronaut mistakenly assumed
that his self-awareness was related to the reflection he
saw in the mirror. When he asked, "Who am I?" the answer he gave himself was, "I am what I see in the mirror."
We, too, make a similar mistake. As we look at ourselves
in a mirror, we attach our sense of I-ness to what we see.
"I am that body," we say. In the same way, we attach our
I-ness to events taking place in our minds, such as when
we think, "I am talented," or "I am depressed." The truth
of the matter, however, is that the body, the talent, the
depression, and everything else around us and within us
do not define the basic I-ness. These things are aspects
of pattern, and pattern lies in the abode of mind. The
creator is the source, the creation is the pattern. You are
the creator. Your ultimate I-ness is the Big I, or the "I am"
that relates to your soul. You are not that which you created. The mistake we all make is that, like the astronaut,
we have come to identify our I-ness with the pattern.
Since the pattern expresses itself in different ways over
life, your sense of "I" changes as you grow older. Your
overall self-concept as a child was different than it is
now. Moreover, you probably don't even remember the
earlier one. In a similar manner, if you accept reincarnation, you have had many self-concepts over many lives,
none of which you remember save the present one. The
perceived continuity of your I-ness during the course of
your present life is illusory, due to the gradual change of
the pattern. In any event, it is through this pattern and
your self-awareness that you come to know your Big I.

Working with ideals facilitates this attunement. One reading puts it like this:

> . . . often the ability to attune self [to the infinite is a result of] habit; for . . . the physical is of the material. The mental or habit forming is of the subconscious, and oft *through* the subconscious *only* may the superconscious be brought into being. 137-127

The "superconscious" mind is closest to the source of your *ideal expression* within the divine pattern. Therefore, working with ideals helps your attunement with it as well as your eventual nonattachment from all patterns. With this comes the transformation of personality and the experience of complete freedom as one's will is aligned with that of God.

Two other practices are encouraged in the readings as one works with ideals. One of these is prayer. This is defined as a conscious effort to communicate with God. There are many reasons people pray. Some prayers are petitionary, others give thanks, and some express adoration. The readings tell us that prayer is talking to God. When we do this, we have to have some idea about Whom or What we are talking to, as well as some sort of viewpoint about spiritual reality. At its most elementary level then, prayer helps us to understand the pattern of creation as we see it and, in so doing, helps us to define our ideals.

Complementary to prayer is meditation. We discussed this earlier as a method of relaxation, but it has another value. On a deeper level, meditation allows us to tune in to our spiritual identities, or Big I's. I use the word *allow* because the experience of this identity is a natural process. While prayer is talking to God, the readings tell us that meditation is listening to Him, and it is this experience that integrates the little I with the Big I. Remember, your true nature incorporates both source and pattern, creator and created, but you experience neither in full. Prayer provides the framework for understanding pattern, while meditation facilitates attunement with its source.

There are many ways to practice deep meditation. The readings emphasize the importance of intent and purpose, or why you want to do this. If your purpose is spiritual becoming, you're on the right track. If it's for curiosity, adventure, or other ego-related goals, meditation can prove dangerous. The reason for this is that meditation accesses various spiritual dimensions or levels of mind. If this is attempted for the wrong reasons, it can lead to dire consequences, ranging from overwhelming fear to serious illness. Since this may be difficult to comprehend, try recalling the last time you had a nightmare and ask yourself where all that fear came from. It had to come from somewhere in you! This is the very fear that can appear, in addition to more serious problems, if meditation is undertaken for the wrong reasons.

At this point you may be wondering if you should practice meditation. The answer lies in your goals. If meditation is to be learned as a simple relaxation technique for the purpose of habit change, there is no harm. For the transformation of personality, however, its goal should embrace spiritual enlightenment. Deep meditation should seek integration of self with Self as an end, not symptom relief. Such relief will naturally accompany your efforts in this direction.

With this in mind, let's now look at procedure. The readings offer specific suggestions here. They recommend first that meditation be preceded by a period of preparation. What does this mean? If you knew that you were about to meet your Big I, which is a tiny replica of God, how would you get yourself ready? The answer here obviously varies from one person to the next, and this is what the readings emphasize. They tell us that we should prepare for meditation in ways that are meaningful for each of us, rather than following a predetermined format. Just as your understanding of God forms the foundation of your spiritual ideal, it should also be the basis of what you consider to be appropriate preparation for meditation. For some, this may involve an elaborate procedure of bathing, bible reading, and the use of adjuncts like music and incense. For others, a simple glass of water may suffice.

Following preparatory procedures, the readings recommend that you sit down and begin your meditation with a prayer. This helps to focus the mind in a spiritual direction and provides the framework for your ideals. Prayer is effective to the extent that it is sincere and spontaneous, rather than something recited by rote. The readings present an interesting elaboration of the value of the Lord's Prayer in this respect.

After the prayer, your attention should be directed to an affirmation. This consists of a word or short phrase that may relate to your spiritual ideal. If your ideal is love, for instance, the affirmation may be, "I am love." The readings often quote the Bible when recommending affirmations, such as, "Be still and know that I am God." Regardless of what you choose, your efforts should be sincere and your feelings those of expectancy. You should concentrate on the affirmation with the belief that it is true and that positive experiences will follow. The readings relate to such experiences as the "still, small voice."

While meditating, you should try to maintain a passive attitude. This means that you should not worry about intrusive thoughts. Such thoughts represent mental habits of your personality. If you attempt to fight them or if you become discouraged by them, you are reacting with yet other habits. Remember that you are attempting to go beyond habit patterns and to tune in to the source of these patterns. To facilitate this, meet intrusive thoughts with an effortless return to your affirmation.

Deep meditation requires patience as well as a determination to be consistent and persistent in your efforts. Try to meditate daily for about twenty minutes. If possible, do this in the same place and at the same time each day. As you begin to see positive results, you may want to increase the amount of time you practice.

Integrating prayer and meditation in working with ideals is an excellent approach to psychological disorders. It is the basis of the psychospiritual approach recommended in the readings. In addressing both immediate and remote causes, it offers the opportunity not only for relief from psychological suffering but for a transformation of personality through spiritual becoming.

10

Planning Your Strategy: What Are Your Goals?

To make the ideal, purpose, aim . . . that which is satisfying the individual purposes . . . is to become selfish, self-centered, purposeless, in the spiritual sense, and self-indulgent in the mental self, and must . . . bring that which makes for unrest, contention, strife . . . for it must be disappointing, for it is not founded in life—which *is constructive* to the *whole,* not for an individual.   Edgar Cayce reading 274-3

Now that we have looked at different self-help strategies for psychological disorders, it is time to make a decision about which approach is right for you. In doing this, the first thing you have to examine are your purposes. What are you seeking to accomplish? The usual answer here is symptom relief, or the end of the distress that is associated with the problem. Your aims may be higher than this, however, as you may wish to avail yourelf of the wealth of information in the readings of Edgar Cayce. Here, you would be seeking the transformation of your personality, in addition to the termination of personal suffering. In this case, your choice of strategy would incorporate working with ideals, prayer, and meditation.

After deciding what your aims are, review your problem analysis list to see what aspect of the disorder you've
chosen to work on first. Recall that the symptoms of a
psychological problem can appear as thoughts, feelings,
and behaviors. Hopefully, you picked one or more of
these that are easy for you to handle. In addition, look
over the antecedants of the symptoms, or the situations
in which they occur. Do the same thing with their consequences, or the rewards and punishments that follow
them.

Next, look at the contract you made with yourself. Up
to this point, it should include the symptom you've chosen to work on, its base rating, and your therapeutic
goals. Now, you want to add a specific coping strategy to
it. The choice of strategy may be determined, to some
extent, by the nature of the symptom. Feelings of anxiety, for instance, can be alleviated by learning to relax.
However, they can also be significantly reduced by the
use of imagination, thought restructuring, and strict behavioral approaches. The better way to choose a coping
strategy, then, is to pick something that feels right for
you. Coordinate it, if you can, to your style of personality. An individual who loves to daydream might find an
imaginal technique more beneficial than a behavioral
one. Another person who is more action-oriented, however, might fare better with the behavioral approach.
Also, a combination of procedures may be more helpful
than using a single one alone. Once you have noted the
strategy you will use, sign your contract. As you begin
the challenge of helping yourself, always remember the
importance of persistence, consistency, and, above all,
patience.

Let's consider a hypothetical situation to help you get
started. Imagine a woman who is extremely dependent,
non-assertive, and unable to make decisions in life. As a

result, she always clings to others and is afraid of being alone. Her dependent personality style makes her very unhappy, and she desperately wants to change. What can she do? In preparing her problem analysis list, she focuses on her non-assertive behavior as a starting point. She monitors the frequency of this behavior, establishes a base rating, and defines a goal for herself. She decides to use positive visualization as her coping strategy.

In one situation, she is seeking only symptom relief. Here, she prepares a mental movie, in which she pictures herself behaving assertively. She acts in her own best interests, without feeling nervous about it. As she does this, others are approving and accepting of her, which serves as positive reinforcement. In another scenario, her aim is personality transformation. In this situation, she begins by setting a spiritual ideal, and then translates it into psychological and behavioral terms. As the ideal is an expression of her individuality, the mental movie she constructs revolves around its theme. Here, she again pictures herself behaving assertively but not based in self-interests. Instead, her assertive actions reflect the love she has both for herself and for others as spiritual beings. In the first situation, the visualization scenario is one of personality and separateness. The second one, on the other hand, represents individuality and oneness. In addition to using positive visualization in this manner, she would also pray for guidance and strength in her endeavors as well as systematically practice meditation.

Let us now turn to see what the readings have to say about specific psychological disorders. As we look at these, the attempt will be made to relate them to the diagnostic criteria outlined in the *Diagnostic and Statistical Manual of Mental Disorders* or DSM-IV.[1] This manual presents criteria for all emotional problems. In most cases, we can never really be sure of the exact diagnoses of the individuals requesting readings from Cayce, either from the psychiatric standards present in his time or those of today. These can only be inferred by the nature of the information given. This is important to keep in mind as we examine these disorders. In most cases, we will be assuming a probable diagnosis based on today's psychiatric standards.

Diagnoses will be linked to Cayce's etiological paradigm. These will incorporate karmic correctives resulting from the misapplications of will by a Big I, beginning with its inception in God and continuing through past lives, astrological sojourns, and present circumstances. General therapeutics will be seen as holistic, addressing mental, physical, and spiritual factors. Psychospiritual therapeutics will focus on the need to work with ideals, prayer, and meditation. These will be coordinated to the psychological strategies we discussed, primarily those of the behavioral orientation. This will enable you to work with the readings in a more efficacious manner.

PART 3

▲

THE APPROACH
OF
EDGAR CAYCE

11

Anxiety Disorders:
Living in Fear

Fear is that element in the character and in the experience of individuals which brings about more of trouble than any other influence in the experience of an entity.

Edgar Cayce reading 2560-1

Fear or anxiety is an emotion we all experience at times, and it can be most uncomfortable. Yet, it is part of life and is often quite useful. If your house is on fire, for instance, the various components of your fear reaction help you to survive. Anxiety has a functional value in situations of danger. It becomes a problem, however, when it is experienced in the absence of such danger. Here, it serves no apparent purpose and is considered to be maladaptive. It takes on many forms, like worry, nervousness, dread, and apprehension, and it affects many areas of personality functioning. It can interfere with your concentration, making thinking more difficult. It can produce bodily reactions like a racing heart, light-headedness, shortness of breath, and nausea. The anxiety can also adversely interfere with your normal everyday routine. Such anxiety reactions underlie a variety of psychological problems called *anxiety disorders.* These are very common conditions, often prompting people to seek out psychotherapy. Let's look at some of them as described in DSM-IV.[1]

One is referred to as a *generalized anxiety disorder.* This is a condition where a person feels extremely anxious, or excessively worried about something such as finances, work, school, family, or other matters. In addition to the feeling of anxiety, the individual may have symptoms like restless sleep, a "blank" mind, muscle tension, jumpiness, fatigue, and irritability. The anxiety is experienced frequently for at least six months and seems uncontrollable. It distresses the individual and can interfere with his or her ability to function on a daily basis.

Another anxiety disorder is the *specific phobia.* In this condition, there is an excessive or unreasonable fear that is triggered by something the individual encounters or expects to encounter. This could be almost anything, such as animals, insects, blood, enclosed places, heights, loud noises, water, and many other stimuli. Even though the phobic person sees that the fear is unreasonable, or that the reaction is extreme, he or she still becomes very anxious when confronting the phobic object and may even have a panic attack. A panic attack is a source of tremendous emotional pain and includes such symptoms as palpitations, perspiration, shakiness, shortness of breath, choking sensations, chest pains, nausea, dizziness, "strange" feelings of unreality regarding one's self and the environment, loss of control, numbness, chills, hot flushes, and fears of going crazy or dying. If possible, the phobic person avoids the source of fear or else endures it with tremendous discomfort. This condition is a source of great distress for the individual and can interfere with everyday activities.

When social anxiety is present, the condition is called a *social phobia.* Here, an individual is overly anxious and may even panic in situations where there are unfamiliar people present or where there is the anticipation of being scrutinized by others. The person is also concerned that the others may notice the anxiety, resulting in humiliation and embarrassment. Because of this, social situations tend to be avoided. If this isn't possible, they are endured with dread. This condition, like the others, causes a great deal of distress and can significantly interfere with one's functioning.

As we can see, in both specific and social phobias, the individual may have panic attacks. There is another anxiety disorder in which such attacks occur repeatedly and come "out of the blue." This is the *panic disorder,* where a person suddenly experiences a sense of impending doom, a feeling that he or she is about to "explode" or "bust." Because the panic attacks are unexpected here, the person worries about where they came from, what effect they will have, and whether there will be additional ones. The problem also significantly affects behavior. Individuals with panic disorders may be so nervous about having these acute attacks of anxiety that they avoid various places, just in case they might occur there. If this is not possible, they may go out only in the safety of family or friends. If they must go out alone, considerable distress is experienced. In these cases, the condition is referred to as a *panic disorder with agoraphobia.*

The final anxiety disorder we'll examine here is the *obsessive-compulsive disorder.* This problem is characterized by either an obsession or a compulsion. Sometimes, both are present. What are these? An obsession is something that seems to *pop* into your head uninvited.

This can be a sexual impulse, as a command to engage in some repulsive sexual act; an aggressive impulse, like harming someone you love; a thought that you will be contaminated by germs; ideas of doubt, for instance, whether or not you locked the front door; images where you feel the urge to organize everything in neat and orderly ways; and many other possibilities. Although obsessive individuals understand that the thoughts they experience originate within their own minds, they feel very anxious about them and attempt to suppress them. While an obsession is an intrusive thought, the compulsion is something the person does over and over, sometimes as a way of dealing with an obsession. For example, obsessions of contamination may lead to compulsive hand washing, while sexual obsessions may result in compulsive praying. The obsessive-compulsive disorder can take up a great deal of the individual's time, cause a lot of distress, and interfere with the normal routine of life. This occurs despite the recognition that the symptoms don't make any sense.

There are numerous instances in the Cayce material where information was requested for problems of anxiety. Whether an individual was suffering from a specific anxiety disorder according to present DSM-IV[2] guidelines would be difficult to say. Nevertheless, it would be safe to assume that some sort of anxiety disorder existed and that this was a primary or secondary reason for the request.

One of the first things that stands out in the readings is the prevalence of anxiety in life and its destructive nature. One reading highlights this by saying:

Fear is the root of most of the ills of mankind . . .
5459-3

This is a very powerful statement. By telling us that

fear is the "root" of most of our problems, we can appreciate its pervasive nature. It relates not only to anxiety disorders but to other psychological problems, physical problems, social problems, in a word, to most of our "ills." The readings trace the remote causes of fear to many factors. They tell us that it originates in an existential anxiety resulting from the initial separation of the Big I from God's pattern of creation. Recall that, as a co-creator with God, each soul was free to express itself. By misapplying its will, it diverged from the divine pattern, and in so doing, lost its true identity of part-within-a-whole. It became more aware of itself as part. In other words, by expressing its identity outside of the divine framework, the Big I weakened its identity with God. The effect of all this was and continues to be fear. One individual is told:

> . . . being afraid is the first consciousness of sin's entering in, for he that is made afraid has lost consciousness of self's own heritage with the Son . . .
> 243-10

The "loss of consciousness" here refers to the weakening of the soul's part-within-a-whole identity, as perfectly expressed by the Christ. This becomes the archetype for the anxiety disorders. The misapplication of will continued as the soul expressed itself through spiritual, mental, and physical patterns. These deviations exacerbated the original separation anxiety and resulted in more conflict. The original cause produced an effect, which in turn served as the cause for another effect, and this as the cause for still another. The process continued in the soul's expression of itself. In our ordinary lives, we are not aware of this conflict, only of its results. What this means is that whatever patterns we created as souls, on any level of reality, exist in us at the present moment as unconscious forces in various degrees of conflict with each other, as well as with the one divine form. The misapplication of will still goes on in our lives whenever we focus on the little I and the self-interests expressed through personality, rather than on the higher ideals of individuality. One reading states this idea very simply:

> *Self*-awareness, *selfishness,* is that that makes men afraid. The awareness of the necessities of the carnal forces in a material world seeking their gratification. 262-29

Recall that the readings define personality as the mask that one wears in society. As such, "gratification" often revolves around your self-image and the concerns you have about what others think of you. The roots of anxiety are thus multifaceted, and the search for etiological factors becomes complex, as one examines immediate and remote causes.

In many cases, the remote causes of anxiety focus on experiences incurred in other earthly lives. Look at the following excerpt suggestive of an obsessive-compulsive disorder:

> *Q. In the present, why do I have the feeling of contamination when touching animals' hair, fur or feathers?*
> A. As in that experience in Atlantis, the thought forces brought into being were of the animal . . . and the *natural* tendency of abhorrence arose from seeing those things take form as menaces, or seeds of indiscretion of beings in the experience . . . *Innately* this appears. 288-29

Here we can see an interesting connection to a former incarnation in Atlantis where the entity witnessed the materialization of menacing animals from thought. What was then a "*natural* tendency of abhorrence" remained as an unconscious memory pattern showing up in the present lifetime as an "innate" contamination obsession.

Another case describes possible elements of a specific phobia:

> Q. Why was I so fearful in early childhood, especially of animals, spiders, and sharp knives—and still dislike to use or to see used a sharp knife?
>
> A. Because of those experiences when thou wert bound about, in those periods in France, when thine associates bound thee for thine virtue, and those activities in the knives, the racks of torture that were all about the entity. 823-1

Here again, negative events from a previous life remained as latent memories, only to reappear as a childhood phobia.

In the following case, another specific phobia is suggested:

> Q. What influence causes me to be afraid of darkness?
>
> A. Those experiences in the activities of the Colonial period; but more particularly from the experiences in the dungeon in which thou wert plunged in France. 852-12

In this case, two separate sets of experiences came together in the present life and manifested as nyctophobia.

The next case appears to be one of hydrophobia. It is traced back to an earlier life in which the individual drowned:

Q. What was the cause of this fear of water?
A. It is from those experiences that brought about destruction to many, in the former appearance. 2428-1

Sometimes, problems of anxiety are linked to experiences that occur between lives. Remember, the readings tell us that life is continuous and that the soul expresses itself in many dimensions symbolized by the sun, moon, and other planets of the solar system. Awareness exists in these realms but in ways that are very different from ordinary consciousness. One reading describes the effects of such an interim experience:

On dark days with little sunshine there is an appreciable manifestation of fear and dread. And especially does this occur when the moon by its position is on the opposite side of the orb or earth. 264-31

At birth, the unconscious patterns associated with previous incarnations and astrological experiences interact with the newly formed pattern of the physical body, as well as with its natural and social environment. This interaction continues throughout life and can be influenced only by one's will. Its effects may precipitate the anxiety disorder. At birth, this is evident in inherent predispositions, while later on in life, it can relate to such factors as traumas, diseases, injuries, and many other occurrences.

The immediate causes of the anxiety disorder, therefore, reflect the present manifestations of patterns in conflict, and these, in turn, come across as imbalances within and between body, mind, and spirit. Usually, all three are involved, as they make up one interdependent system. For instance, if anxiety is centered around conflicting mental habit patterns, this could impact both the spiritual and physical side of the system, which could then produce a secondary reaction in the mind. This, in turn, could have subsequent spiritual and/or physical ramifications resulting in a continuous back-and-forth process. The same thing can happen if the anxiety is centered primarily in physiological or spiritual factors.

An example of mind-body interaction can be seen in the following comments where a person is told that her physical problems are created:

> . . . not so much by the physical inactivity of organs or of the active forces *in* the functioning of the system, as of the *mental* destructive forces created by worry. Worry and fear being, then, the greatest foes to *normal* healthy physical body, turning the assimilated forces in the system into poisons that must be eliminated, rather than into life giving vital forces for a physical body. 5497-1

In another reading, Cayce shows this same idea in reverse, where anxiety is a reaction to physiological disturbance rather than its cause. Here, a person asks whether his anxiety neurosis was the result of childhood fears, as he was told by psychoanalysts. The reading tells him that:

> . . . this condition does *not* arise from those sources intimated. Rather in days back there was an injury in the right side from being struck by a bat or clout of some nature. 3318-1

This injury, in turn, resulted in:

> . . . hindrances causing the blocking of the coordination of the sympathetic and cerebrospinal

nerves with the general mental reaction; almost causing spasmodic reactions or "fits." 3318-1

Not only did the reading trace the anxiety to physiological dysfunction but also added that it was exacerbated by the professional advice he was getting:

> ... there are disturbing conditions, but these to a great extent have arisen from the fear that has been created by what the body has been told is the source of his disturbance. Don't believe 'em! 3318-1

Just as the mind and body interact in the anxiety disorder, so do the other aspects of the spiritual system. The composite picture is, therefore, complex and requires holistic intervention as the attempt is made to bring the total system into alignment. Perhaps the best way to illustrate the therapeutics of the readings is to look at an entire reading. In a letter sent to Cayce, a man writes:

> "Ever since I was a boy, I have been afflicted with a stage fright complex. Psychiatrists say I was shocked badly when real young, and that if the situation could be recalled it would help to dissolve my trouble. This fear has come to bother me in many other ways. Perhaps a reading might help solve the trouble." 5123-1 Reports

From this letter, as well as others he sent, this individual appeared to be suffering from a social phobia, which he described as being "the bane of my whole life." He also indicated that he had tuberculosis. The reading begins by commenting on the chronicity of his problems:

As we find, from longstanding conditions the

body is itself's own enemy. These are conditions where lack of control of the emotions, and the activity of organs through the body by those drainages from the system of the vitality that goes to make for regeneration and the activity in the body, has gradually brought on a complication of disorders through the mental reactions and the physical conditions. 5123-1

Notice here how the social phobia relates to a "complication of disorders." Psychological factors are linked to the individual's "lack of control of the emotions." Physiological factors are evident in the body's lack of energy. The interaction of these is seen "through the mental reactions." No mention is made of repressed childhood memories. As the reading continues, physiological causes are again noted, as well as the lack of spiritual direction:

Weakness in the general vitality of the body, lack of stability in the purposes or desires of the body; all of these become a part of the general conditions. 5123-1

Next, holistic therapeutic recommendations are given. As can be seen, they are centered in a spiritual basis and begin with psychospiritual advice:

As we find, first there must be, if there would be helpful forces for this body, the changes of the mental attitude toward self, toward general surroundings. There must be the holding to some general creative energies, for the body will gain much more by trying and in helping someone else, rather than pitying or excusing or condemning things in others.

That should be the first general change, or attitude of the body, if there would be any permanent help. 5123-1

The advice here is most interesting. Here is a person with an apparent social phobia, who is told that the best way to help himself is through altruism, rather than "pitying or excusing or condeming things in others." This should be uppermost in his mind. It is the primary element in treating the physiological aspect of his condition, as seen here:

For those disturbances in self which cause drainages must be eliminated by trying to do something, either mentally or physically, for someone else. 5123-1

Once the psychospiritual orientation is established, the individual is given various physical therapeutics aimed at fostering a balance of his body, mind, and spirit. These include electrotherapy, osteopathy, and dietary recommendations:

Then, we would commence with the deep therapy treatments given with the deep therapy electrical machines. These should be those that control the activities through the solar plexus, as well as the general reactions through the body. We would have these treatments about once a week, while twice a week we would have osteopathic treatments.
As to diet: We would have more raw vegetables, as well as a very mild meat; such as fish, fowl and lamb, and none of them fried; rather broiled, baked or the like would be better way of preparation. 5123-1

The reading then points out how the physical therapeutics will enable the individual to gain the strength needed to express his altruistic, creative nature:

> If these suggestions are kept up, we will find there will soon grow sufficient strength for the body not to remain in bed through necessity, but will have strength and may be in the open air and active with its hands and mind toward some creative activity. 5123-1

Next, the individual asks the sleeping Cayce what his fear is due to, and how he may overcome it. The response summarizes the etiological factors, as well as underscores the need for spiritual application:

> Q. *What is the cause of my mental fear, and how may I overcome it?*
> A. As has been indicated, the draining of drosses in the system from self-indulgence, and if there is the replacing of such with study, and the applying of self in the physical and mental towards helping others, we can dismiss this fear and tension in body and build up through the activities as have been given.
> We are through with this body. 5123-1

The "self-indulgence" mentioned here relates to the individual's tendency to pity, excuse or condemn others as pointed out earlier in the reading. These are ego or personality traits and are to be replaced with creative, selfless endeavors.

This reading can serve as a model of the basic view taken by Cayce on the anxiety disorders. The causes are multifaceted, and the treatments holistic. Physical therapeutics are more general, or nonspecific, when there is no significant pathology present or the problem is in the dis-ease phase. If such pathology is evident and the problem represents a disease, it is more debilitating, and physical recommendations more specific. Whatever the phase is, physical therapeutics involve the use of osteopathy, physiotherapy, electrotherapy, diet, and exercise among others. An excellent analysis of this is provided by McMillin.[3]

The psychospiritual therapeutics are usually nonspecific and often repeated for a variety of anxiety disorders. They strongly emphasize a need to establish a spiritual, creative standard of reference in life and to express this through constructive, selfless habit patterns in both attitude and behavior. Establishing spiritual standards means setting spiritual ideals. One woman, who may have been suffering from a generalized anxiety disorder, is told:

One that is at times easily worried at material things. One that at times worries as respecting the application others make of their abilities. In the matter of worry this—in the last analysis—is that of fear. Fear is an enemy to the mental development of an entity changing or wavering the abilities of an entity in many directions . . .

Find that, that is the answer ever for self, as to *an* ideal to be worked toward, to be used at all times, to be leaned upon in adversity and in criticism, in successes, in failures, in pleasures, in hardships, in adversity and in those conditions that are as entanglements of the mental or physical being. 2502-1

While ideals can take many forms, we saw earlier that the readings are Christ-centered. Individuals were repeatedly encouraged to use Jesus as the perfect exemplar and to identify with the pattern expressed through

Him. One man is told:

> Fears arise. If thou hast centered thy choice in
> self, be fearful! If thou art centering self in Him . . .
> then be *not* afraid! 707-1

In setting a spiritual ideal, the readings also stress its
application in both thought, as a mental ideal, and in
deed, as a physical ideal. What this means is that the
spiritual ideal has to become a significant part of one's
life. It has to permeate one's being. To accomplish this,
new habit patterns have to be learned. Such learning requires replacing destructive patterns based on ego and
personality with more constructive ones that reflect the
Big I and individuality. How does one go about develop-
ing new patterns of attitude and behavior? How do you
replace old habits with new ones? We'll answer these
questions by looking at the psychospiritual advice given
in the readings and coordinate it to psychological strategies. In this way, you can deal with your anxiety problem
in the most efficacious manner.

Let's begin by looking at behavior. The readings often
recommend working at this level and changing one's
deeds in a more positive direction. One reading puts it
this way:

> As has been given, know thy Ideal, in what thou
> hast believed; and then act in that manner, minis-
> tering to others. For perfect love casteth out fear,
> and fear can only be from the material things that
> soon must fade away. 1175-1

The emphasis here is on action, on doing something
constructive. This is a recurrent theme in the readings as
a way of coping with the anxiety disorder. One person is
told:

Let that which causes doubt or fear be taken up in the willingness, the desire, to be of help to others. 69-4

Another is advised that anxiety would be eliminated:

By going out and doing something for somebody else; that is, those not able to do for themselves, making others happy, forgetting self entirely . . . in helping someone else you'll get rid of your feelings. 5226-1

In still another case, the individual is told to make kindness a habitual hobby:

Then . . . make it a habit, make it a hobby, to at least each day, speak kindly to someone less fortunate than self. Not that there should be so much the contribution to organized charity, but have those charities of self [that] you never speak of, by speaking kindly to someone each day.

This will let the body rest at night when it hasn't been able to, with its mental and material worries. 5177-2

One of the most effective ways to develop new behavior patterns is to work with positive reinforcement. As we saw earlier, this involves linking the behavior with some reward. This can be material, like treating yourself to a night out, or social, as in the approval of significant others, or even spiritual, as in intuitively knowing that you're doing the right thing. In working with altruistic behavior patterns, you can make these rewards contingent upon helping people or making them happy. Look at the spiritual reward evident in the following comments:

Let fear, let worry, be lost in thy service to others for His name's sake. Let thy heart be lifted up, that ye may hear that "Well done" from Him, who is mindful of those who seek His face. 281-61

In this next reading, the emphasis is on the reinforcing quality of peace and quietness:

Put self rather, then, in the hands, in the mind, of the *Divine* from within, and not attempting, not *trying* to be good, to be kind, to be thoughtful—but just *be,* and *consecrate* self to the service of others. This peace, this quietness that will come within self from such, will find a ready answer in the mind, in the heart, in the life, in the expression of those— every one—whom the body contacts. 5563-1

In the next excerpt, the reinforcing qualities of love and friends is evident:

Show thyself lovely, that ye may have love in thine experience. Not as a possession but as a gift to thy fellow man. Show thyself friendly with the unfriendly, that ye may have friends. 1298-1

In addition to suggesting direct behavior changes in line with one's spiritual ideal, the readings often recommend stimulus control, or putting oneself in situations where such changes can be facilitated. One example of this is bibliotherapy. Cayce often recommends reading inspirational material as a self-help technique. While the readings suggest many helpful sources, the most frequent, by far, is the Bible. Moreover, they usually suggest the same biblical passages again and again. For instance, a woman who appeared to be suffering from a panic disorder is directed first to the:

. . . thirtieth chapter of Deuteronomy. Read this with the knowledge and realization, as it is assimilated (not merely read but assimilated), that it is self that is being spoken of, as to the sources of consciousness, of awareness, of awakening, of promise.

As this is assimilated, then turn to the words of Him—in the 14th, 15th, 16th, 17th chapters of St. John—for He is the truth, the light, and the light of men—whose assurance and whose promises may be so much a part of self. For He, being the Way, being the water of life—if ye take hold upon the promises there, they will indeed give refreshment to the mind, to the body, and that assurance to the soul of self that He indeed is thy brother! 2114-1

Notice here how the woman is told that the biblical references apply to her, personally. Moreover, she is advised to not only read them, but to "assimilate" them into her life. What are these passages saying? In Deuteronomy 30, the mercy of God is illustrated, as free will is aligned to the pattern of one's individuality, as opposed to the pattern of separateness seen in personality. The passages from John portray the actualization of this pattern in the Christ, as well its relationship to one's individuality. The woman is told that her anxiety disorder would dissipate as these ideas became ideals and permeated her life.

Similar advice is given to another individual, as can be seen in the following comments:

Q. What causes the fears with which I am obsessed at the present time and how can I overcome them?

A. Only by changing the mental attitude . . . if the mental attitude is set much in the way and manner as may be best obtained from the 14th chapter of

St. John, it would be the better. Read that before retiring. Read that when *any* fears come about; we will
find a different attitude! 843-8

In addition to bibliotherapy, the readings recommend
other forms of stimulus control. A reading given for a
four-year-old girl advises that she:

. . . be kept away from fear, away from loud
noises, darkness, the scream of sirens, the shouts of
individuals of fear to the entity. 3162-1

Another reading recommends that the individual's
social environment include:

. . . those who will talk more patiently with him,
those who will take this body for a walk for interesting him in things which have long been neglected
in the life. 5318-1

Still another reading for a twelve-year-old girl advises
those responsible for her to:

Keep those things about the body that make for
the more cheerful reactions. 623-11

In addition to stimulus control and positive reinforcement, the recommendations of the readings can readily
be reconciled with the other psychological strategies,
including in vivo desensitization, exposure, and aversion techniques. Let's now see how the Cayce material
uses the power of imagination, or as the readings put it,
the "imaginative forces." Look at how Cayce answers this
question:

Q. What can I do to relieve myself of the feeling in

the dark of something near, which prevents normal sleep?

A. Surround self in thought with that which may be near in every activity that can only be helpful, sustaining; maintaining such an attitude through the mental and imaginative forces will overcome these conditions. 578-3

This individual, who appeared to be suffering from nyctophobia, was essentially advised to practice positive visualization as a way of dealing with her fears. This technique can be used to work with any form of anxiety. As we saw, it involves the construction of a mental movie depicting a situation that is free of fear. This could very well take the form of seeing oneself surrounded by "helpful" people, events, activities, and things of this sort. The use of spiritual imagery in visualization is often recommended in the readings. This can be seen in the case of another person who also seemed to be suffering from a specific phobia:

Q. How can I overcome my horror of noise and thunderstorms? (I was always afraid of noise, but the fear of thunder has been only in the last 15 or 20 years. If I did not have this, I could manage better.)

A. . . . Surround thyself at such times with the consciousness of a walk and talk with Him, and noise and fear will be no more. 3161-1

In working with positive visualization, the mental movie that is constructed should be as detailed as possible and incorporate many senses and emotions. It might also end with a short affirmation related to peace, serenity, and things of this sort.

Working with imagination can also take the form of covert modeling. Here, you would create a scenario in which you see yourself acting like someone who deals with fear better than you do. This person would serve as your role model, and in your fantasy, you would attempt to identify with him or her. To strengthen the identification, the scenario might include some sort of reward. Since the readings are Christ-centered, they often recommend Jesus as a role model. This is evident in the counseling Cayce gives the following individual:

> Q. *How can I overcome the countless fears which seem to dominate my whole existence?*
> A. . . . Only in Him, knowing—as He has given, "Ye abide in me and I in you, and I will cast out fear." 1058-1

This advice can easily be incorporated into a covert modeling scenario where Jesus is imagined confronting a threatening situation, and you, in turn, merge with His reaction.

In addition to covert modeling, working with imagination can also take place during pre-sleep. The use of hypnagogic suggestion is occasionally recommended in the readings for problems of anxiety. Look at how Cayce answers the following question:

> Q. *Why does my daughter [5043] have such a fear of water, and what can I do to eliminate this fear?*
> A. It may only be eliminated by the suggestions that may be made as the daughter turns to sleep. *Make* the suggestions as for the usefulness of water in the experience, else we may have indeed a barren body. 2428-1

As you can see, the advice is directed to changing the fear at its root, by replacing a negative association to water with a more positive one. In addition to using imagination through positive visualization, covert modeling, and pre-sleep suggestions, other imaginative strategies can easily be incorporated into the Cayce therapeutics.

Let's now look at another psychospiritual technique of the readings, that of using reason to restructure thinking patterns. The use of the rational mind to effect lifestyle changes requires a challenge to twisted patterns that are rooted in personality. Replacing them with more altruistic and selfless patterns is a constant theme of the readings as seen in the following comments:

> To lose self to such fears is to keep self busy in contemplation of the good that may be accomplished in loving appreciation, loving thought, of how there may be meted to someone those things that have been and are enjoyed by self, in little material things, greater mental things, and the glorious spiritual attributes of every soul. 1928-1

Individuals with anxiety disorders often harbor various irrational beliefs. One of them relates to the finality and devastation experienced when things in life don't turn out as expected. A reasonable alternative to this belief is to look at life as a challenge and to attempt to make bad things better. If this is impossible, moreover, it is best to resign one's self to life, rather than to fight it on the grounds that it is horrible. The readings not only agree with this but go much deeper. They tell us that most things in life are turning out exactly as expected:

> Little happens *just* by chance—though there are accidents, even in creation. 255-6

Furthermore, we are constantly meeting ourselves in life. Anxiety disorders are the effects of previous actions, occurring in this dimension or in others, whether in the immediate past or in the distant past. One person is told:

> Each soul finds itself in body, in mind, in that place in which it—itself, as an entity, as a whole—is meeting only its own self! 1632-2

The entity that took these actions could be the present "you" or another "you" that you do not remember. This idea is highlighted in the following reading:

> What ye sow, ye reap. Apparently there are often experiences in which individuals reap that which they have not sown—but this is only the short self vision of the entity . . . 2528-3

So, if things in life don't turn out as expected, rather than viewing them as hindrances and feeling dread and anxiety, we should look at them as opportunities to more fruitful and productive ends. Another irrational belief often seen in anxiety disorders is the idea that they are caused by outside influences, related to people, situations, events, etc. The rational comeback here is to focus, not on external sources, but instead on one's interpretation of these sources. In other words, events don't produce anxiety. It results, instead, from what we say to ourselves about these events. Again, the readings agree with this, but view it within a larger perspective. They tell us that many of our thought patterns result from previous actions based on ego and self-interests. These patterns are habitual and produce negative emotions, one of which is anxiety. To deal with these patterns, the readings recommend that we base all our thoughts in a spiritual premise, and as these take hold of our lives, more positive emotions will follow. This can be seen in the following comments:

Reason, then, in self, from that angle—"*I am* His—God's. He *is* mindful of me. And in applying His nature, His service, I may better serve my fellow man to the glory of Him who gives me life, light and immortality."

That is the approach of the attitude. 2952-1

Another psychospiritual strategy mentioned in the readings is relaxation. Look at how Cayce answers the following question:

Q. *What should I do to ease nervous condition?*
A. Just relaxing of the body at regular periods is the best. This is much better than depending upon outside influences. Extra amounts of B-1 vitamin taken will be the better way and manner, but perfect relaxation [is the best remedy]. Have a period when you forget everything . . . 3120-2

Notice that the reading is recommending relaxation over external therapeutics other than vitamins. In addition, it points out that relaxing the body will ease the nervous condition or relax the mind. This is very much in line with progressive muscle relaxation. One could also learn to relax by using other techniques like self-hypnosis or light meditation.

As we can see, Cayce's readings offer a variety of approaches for dealing with disorders of anxiety, all of which are reconcilable with the psychological strategies we discussed. The readings always approach the problem holistically and recommend that you work with ideals. On a psychospiritual level this means changing habits of mind and behavior to effect more constructive lifestyle patterns based in selflessness. While still habitual in nature, these patterns serve as catalysts to facilitate a disengagement from all habits as free will is increased. This is a natural outcome as one becomes more aligned with the true nature of spiritual essence.

The readings also offer additional means of help. Relief from anxiety can come through laughter, hobbies, interests, careers, and exercise. One reading focuses on laughter and tells the individual:

> Remember that a good laugh, an arousing even to . . . hilariousness, is good for the body, physically, mentally, and gives the opportunity for greater mental and spiritual awakening. 2647-1

Finally, and most important, the readings advise incorporating prayer and deep meditation with the psycho-spiritual approach one takes in working with ideals. The benefit of prayer is seen rather dramatically in these comments:

> . . . remember the injunction—never worry as long as you can pray. When you can't pray—you'd better begin to worry! For then you have something to worry about! 3569-1

In another reading, Cayce suggests a specific prayer to be used in dealing with the anxiety:

> When fear of the future occurs, or fear of the past, or fear of what others will say—put all such away with this prayer, not merely by mouth, not merely by thought, but in body, in mind and in soul say:
> *"Here am I, Lord—Thine! Keep me in the way Thou would have me go, rather than in that I might choose."* 2540-1

Prayer is a powerful tool for effecting positive changes in life and can be easily integrated with any psychological strategy. The same is true for deep meditation. As we have seen, this is a complementary procedure to prayer. One is talking to God and the other is listening to Him. In one reading, the individual is told to:

> *Open* thine inner self, thine inner abilities, to the glories of how the Father through the Son may work in and through thee; for perfect love in Him casteth out fear. For, when each soul may see that whereunto it has been called, through the perfecting of itself in body, in mind, in His name, it may be His channel for blessings to others. In this manner cast out fear. 513-1

However you decide to work with the Cayce material is, of course, entirely up to you. It would be advantageous to choose a strategy that fits in with your style of personality, so that it is more natural for you. Remember, also, the benefits of writing things down. With the preparation of a problem analysis list, a target symptom, and goals, select your psychospiritual strategy and indicate everything in a contract. As always, be persistent, consistent, and above all, patient as you work on your anxiety disorder.

12

Depression: When Sad Feelings Won't Go Away

Q. What is behind my feeling of depression and discouragement?

A. . . . these feelings arise from the self-effacement that is self-condemnation. Condemn not others, and not thyself. Leave that thou canst not do nor understand to *Him,* who is the Giver of all good and perfect gifts. For in Him ye live and move and have thy being. Do not engage, in mind or body, in that which brings condemnation to self.

Edgar Cayce reading 2116-2

Another common psychological disorder is depression. Depression is a form of sadness, which many of us have felt at some point in life. Often, it is associated with some loss. The obvious example that comes to mind is the death of a loved one. Sometimes, sadness occurs during what should be happy times. The "holiday paradox," for example, refers to the blues that many people experience during the Christmas season. In addition, some people feel sad when new events enter their lives, like beginning college, getting a new job, changing a residence, marriage, having a baby, and so on. Others feel sad when things end, like finishing school, getting divorced, retiring, and events of this sort. In all these situations, sadness is precipitated by some external happening. It is a reaction to these events. Some people, however, feel down for no apparent reasons. Sadness becomes a depressive disorder when it meets certain diagnostic criteria.

The DSM-IV[1] describes depression as a type of *mood disorder*. This is a condition where your feelings represent an exaggerated version of a normal mood. For example, you may be feeling okay, and then become sad at some point. If the sadness were to get severe and you had additional symptoms as well, you might be a candidate for a unipolar depression. Another possibility is that the depression alternates with exaggerated feelings of well-being, euphoria, and mania. Here, the possibility for a *bipolar disorder* exists.

There are two main types of unipolar depression. In what is referred to as a *major depressive disorder,* the individual experiences a major depressive episode. Here, in addition to feeling depressed, the person may have no interest in anything, complain about sleep problems or appetite disturbances, feel tired all the time, feel worthless and guilty, be unable to think clearly, show agitated or retarded patterns of behavior, and think a lot about death or suicide. If five of these symptoms are present for at least two weeks, and one of them is either a feeling of depression or a loss of interest in things, the problem is considered a major depressive disorder. This can occur just once in a person's life, or again and again, with normal periods of at least two months between episodes.

Another unipolar depression is the *dysthymic disorder*. Here, a major depressive episode does not occur. Instead, the individual feels depressed much of the time for at least two years. In addition, two other symptoms have to be present, including appetite disturbances, sleep problems, fatigue, low self-esteem, concentration difficulties, and feelings of hopelessness. As you can see, there is considerable overlap between these two conditions. The main difference between them is whether or not a major depressive episode occurs.

Cayce gave many readings for people complaining of depression. As we noted with the anxiety disorders, it is difficult to diagnose these individuals based on current DSM-IV[2] diagnostic criteria. Nevertheless, we are going to assume that a form of depressive disorder existed, and this was a primary or secondary reason for requesting the reading.

Of all the symptoms associated with depression, the readings emphasize the destructive nature of low self-esteem, or feelings of worthlessness. They refer to this as self-condemnation and make a very interesting point about it. They tell us that self-condemnation is really a condemnation of God. The reason for this is that when you condemn your little I, you are in essence also condemning your Big I, since one is linked to the other. The Big I, moreover, represents God in you. One individual is told that discouragement brings:

> . . . periods when the entity becomes oppressed; and begins to condemn self; *forgetting* that in condemning self there is that giving of expression which belittles the Divine within. 1089-8

What are the roots of depression? As with the anxiety disorders, its archetype lies in an existential conflict resulting from the misapplication of will by the Big I. This becomes convoluted through the soul's expression in various states of mind and appears as different symptoms of the depressive disorder. Many readings point to past-life factors as additional causative factors in the etiology of the problem.

In one case, a woman's depression is traced to actions she took in a previous lifetime related to the witch trials in Salem, Massachusetts. During this life, she was apparently very intolerant of people who were interested in spiritualism and the ability to communicate with the deceased. Her reading points out that she:

> ... caused many hardships. When some of those were ducked, the entity was present and gave consent. When some were beaten with many strikes, the entity gave evidence and consent to such. Hence in the present the entity finds itself bound with those periods when consciousness is not able to wholly attain or gained. 3630-2

Having instilled hopelessness in others, she was now witnessing the corrective effect of this through her own depression. In another case, a woman was shown how her present symptoms of worthlessness and confusion related to activities in a previous life:

> Before this, then, we find the entity was in the land of its present nativity, during those periods when there were the disturbances between the North and South in the land of nativity.
>
> Then entity was one who acted in the capacity of finding and indicating information which would be beneficial or helpful for one of the sides in that undertaking. This in itself brought into the entity's experience that which was oft condemning.
>
> Thus we find in its own experience in the present, irrespective of what others have said, the entity condemns self; though in the same breath may be boasting of that it is capable of accomplishing. And these have brought about experiences or things of the nature that have apparently been underhand,

in comparison to the entity's better activity or development. For what ye sowed, ye also will reap. As ye have confused, ye will be confused. 2160-1

In addition to highlighting events in previous lives as causative factors in depression, the readings often provided information regarding astrological sojourns. Look at how one such experience relates to a woman's self-consciousness and low self-esteem:

The Uranian influence, as it is understood, makes for the exception, or the extremes, or the interest in those things not liked, desired, or influencing the regular or ordinary individual; hence these that have been called idiosyncrasies at times of the body in the present experience have made for a self-consciousness that tends to make those conditions where self-condemnation has arisen. 1928-1

This woman's "idiosyncrasies" were related to experiences she had in the state of consciousness associated with Uranus. These were apparently offensive to other people, making her self-conscious and causing her esteem to be deflated.

In the next case, the individual's personality is affected by three astrological states of consciousness:

We find in Mercury the reasoning, and yet this is so tempered with Neptune and Uranus as for the entity to oft become too easily influenced by what others will say . . .

These then are the promptings that are deep within, that oft find self-condemnation because of what others may say. 2540-1

Notice again how low self-esteem is related to an interpretation of how others will react. This is quite usual in life, since, as we have seen, the readings define personality as the masks we wear for others to see. How we come across to others, then, is very important; and in individuals predisposed to depression, it can be a major concern.

The interaction of patterns from the origin of the soul through previous lives and astrological sojourns interfaces with the birth of the physical body and can predispose an individual to depression at any point in life. The following case, which is suggestive of a bipolar disorder, focuses on the role of heredity. The individual is told that:

> . . . while there are physical disturbances which prevent the better normal reactions, in giving the causes and their effects upon the physical body much of that which is a part of the heritage of the mental *and* physical must be taken into consideration. 1614-1

Whether or not a depressive disorder occurs depends on the interplay of this "heritage" with various environmental factors like stress, accidents, injuries, and many other possibilities. This is also affected, of course, by the action of one's free will. The interaction of patterns is always seen in the readings.

One woman's depression, for instance, is related to:

> . . . the aftereffect of conditions from childbirth . . . 964-1

Another is told that her condition relates to:

> . . . a natural consequence of changes that are coming about in the physical forces of the body . . .

Hence, as we find, these are those disturbing conditions that arise from the menopause period and the natural accompanying conditions of same . . . And these periods of melancholia, the periods of the inability to sleep . . . those disturbing forces in the digestive system, those tendencies for the body to become overexcited and overanxious . . . 1133-1

A teenage girl is told how her problems:

. . . may have been produced by an injury or fall in a much earlier period. 1845-1

The part of the body affected was her spine. This was also the case for another woman who is told that her depression arose:

. . . primarily from physical conditions that exist in the body from a hurt—or injury—to the coccyx end of the spine . . . 2325-1

In some cases, the environmental precursors to the depressive disorder reflected interpersonal factors. This is evident in the following reading where a man's depression is:

. . . brought about by the feeling of resentments from those who should have been very kind and very patient and very reluctant to have ever put this body where there wouldn't be the little gentlenesses and kindnesses daily administered. 5318-1

In another case, depression results from an earlier repression:

... of a specific nerve shock to the body, both from a physical and moral and a psychological effect that was produced in the body ... 411-1

One interesting situation traces part of a woman's depression to her attempts to meditate at times when her body was unprepared for doing so. The reading indicates that:

... there has been the inclination for the body, through activities of the mental self in its anxiety, to raise or open the centers of the body through meditation and activity when the physical forces were not in the condition for such. 1749-1

As we can see, the etiology of depression, like that of anxiety, is complex and relates to many remote and more immediate causes. These causes can affect the person at the spiritual, mental, or physical level, or at any combination of these. Moreover, even though depression is a psychological experience, it doesn't have to be centered in the mind, per se. It may reflect a reaction of the mind to factors originating in the body or in the spirit. Since the three are interdependent, all are usually involved in the total picture of the disorder which is viewed as a system in conflict. In many readings, depression was seen as primarily a physical problem that was affecting the mind. McMillin[3] provides an excellent examination of the physiological factors mentioned by Cayce. These related to nervous system incoordinations, toxemia, disturbed circulation, and glandular dysfunctions. The following case exemplifies this in a woman whose depression was caused by spinal subluxations preventing her body from normal functioning, and:

... have much to do with the nervous spells [also

the melancholia spells] that come to the body in various forms of cycle functioning of the organism. The subluxations we find are in the 8th and 9th dorsal, and in the 4th lumbar . . . these conditions as exist in nerve system, often bring to the body those of that of the depression that causes little things to become very large in the mental image of the body, and the body takes the body-mental images as realities when they are only imaginations of the entity's own making. 4568-1

Notice the word "imaginations" here, and the possibility that the reading was referring to possible cognitive errors of magnification or jumping to conclusions ("little things to become very large").

The focus on physical etiological factors or causations in many of the readings expanded the strict view of psychological origins held at that time and to a large extent today. This is emphasized in the following case:

Now, in the physical forces of the body we find there are conditions that nominally would be called purely *mental*. We have conditions that, viewed from the psychiatrist standpoint, are of a *mental*. We have conditions as viewed from the psychoanalytical condition would be called suppression; yet these are *not* correct, yet all would be correct.

In the condition then existent, we find there are physical functionings that have been not so much suppressed as so *overtaxed* as to cause enlargements that produce in the functioning of the sympathetic and cerebrospinal system those of incoordination, or not proper returns from impulse; or that of *fear* supplanted often by that of depression following same. 4432-1

— While many readings viewed depression as stemming from physiological dysfunctions, others saw it as primarily psychological in origin and related to various destructive attitudinal habit patterns. These patterns reflected anger, condemnation, disappointments, rejections, loneliness, resentments, regrets, remorse, and many others. These usually were correlated with low self-esteem. Although centered in the mind, such patterns had detrimental effects on the body. We can see this in the next case, which contains general information on the physical effects of low self-esteem:

> In giving an interpretation of the disturbance as we find here, the mental attitude has as much to do with the physical reactions as illnesses in the body. For as we find, in the physical or purely pathological little disturbs the body, save sympathetically, but in the mental attitude there is so much of the making for the degrading of self that self-destruction becomes a part of the reaction, but it is wholly mental. And thus the nerve forces for the body, this body as any body, any individual, who makes destructive thought in the body, condemning self for this or that, will bring, unless there are proper reactions, dissociation or lack of coordination between sympathetic and cerebrospinal system, and it may develop any condition which may be purely physical by deterioration of mental processes and their effect upon organs of the body. 5380-1

In many cases of depression, the readings centered the problem in both physiological and psychological factors, as in the following:

> Now, as we find, there are abnormal conditions that disturb the better physical functioning of the

body. Some of these are the natural result of the mental attitudes; some are the attempts of the body-physical to adjust itself to the changes that come about in the physical activities of the body. And the combination of these makes for a disturbance that is not wholly mental nor wholly physical, but a psychopathic as well as a pathological effect—that produces the complications and disturbances. 770-1

In still other readings, the depression was more related to spiritual factors. In one case, a woman was told that her interpersonal attitudes did not measure up to her spiritual ideal, and, as a result, her self-esteem was deflated. Look at how the reading answers her question:

> Q. Why do I feel, in a way, at war with myself so much and so often?
> A. Because there is not at all times other than self-condemnation in the feelings that are held respecting others or their attitude. This makes the experiences in the position of *incoordinating* with that ideal that is claimed by self. 538-33

As with the anxiety disorders, we can see that the Cayce approach to depression is multifaceted. Immediate causes reflect more remote ones and appear as symptoms through an interaction of body, mind, and spirit. Holistic therapeutics attempt to engage the will of the individual to form new habit patterns at all levels of this systemic conflict. To appreciate this, let's now look at a complete reading for depression. It was given for a twenty-four-year-old woman who indicated she was sad, had no drive, had lost her interests in life, and was experiencing a great deal of fatigue. The reading begins by placing her psychological conflict within a spiritual context. It advises her to look at her body, mind, and spirit as one system and to consider her problem as an imbalance within this system:

> Now as we find in considering the particular disturbances which exist with this body—and these with the view of bringing normalcy and a revivifying of purposes, desires or ambitions—the body *whole* must be taken into consideration; that is, the physical, the mental, and the spiritual attributes of the body.
>
> For while each of the phases of a body-development is met within its own environ or phase, there are experiences which arise within a body—as we find within this body—when all of these must be considered as they coordinate or cooperate one with another.
>
> And as is then to be understood, these *must* coordinate and cooperate—body, mind, soul—if there is to be the best reaction in the physical, mental or spiritual.
>
> Hence the injunction—from the spiritual aspects, and O that every soul would gain the concept, know and be conscious within—that "The Lord Thy God Is ONE!" 1189-2

The spiritual framework of oneness is given in the last paragraph here as something we should all look at. The reading continues by considering the woman's problem as an interaction of psychological and spiritual elements:

> Now with this body we find there has been an exceeding upset in the ideals of the body-mind; coming from disappointments in individuals and in the

reaction to that which is the ideal of the entity within itself. 1189-2

This individual apparently was disappointed in other people because they didn't measure up to her ideals. As we'll see later on, she apparently gave in to the wishes of others in order to keep their respect. This incongruity produced her psychological distress:

And being of a supersensitive nature, it has (the mental) *rebelled* at these conditions. 1189-2

The psychological "rebellion" in turn produced biological malfunctions resulting in her depression:

Now the expressions of these reactions are within the *physical* forces of the body.

Hence we have been gradually on the border of a nervous breakdown, as it would be called by most pathologists or psychologists.

Yet through the emotions these have produced, as we find, *definite* reactions in the physical forces of the body; as related to the nervous system, both cerebrospinal and sympathetic. And those areas that find greater distress are where the cerebrospinal and the sympathetic or imaginative centers coordinate with the physical reactions of the body.

Hence we have had periods of uncontrollable melancholy. We have had periods of the uncontrollable overflow of the ducts that express emotions; inability of perfect assimilation—which immediately upsets the catabolism of the whole physical body.

These then, as we find, are both pathological and psychological conditions that disturb the equilibrium of the body. 1189-2

After examining the immediate causes of the problem, the reading continues with holistic therapeutic recommendations, focusing first on her spiritual ideals:

These are not as faults, these are not as conditions that may not be corrected; yet—from the very nature of their affectation through the emotions—both the physical *and* the mental are to be taken into consideration in giving counsel or advice for corrective forces for this body.

First: *Who* is to say as to what must be any individual's ideal? But know, O Soul, that it must be founded in spiritual, unseen, everlasting things! What are these? Faith, hope, love; without thought of self. For when self or the own ego becomes disappointed, know that you have been disappointing *in* your relationships to that which produces or may produce same. 1189-2

The woman is advised to focus her ideals around altruistic spiritual themes grounded in faith, hope, and love. Her present ideals were apparently not high enough or not spiritually based. As a result, she experienced many disappointments. Perhaps these ideals reflected remote events in her distant past where she disappointed others, and she was now experiencing karmic effects in real ways or through a distorted interpretation of events.

The reading continues in further describing the inherent nature of the true spiritual ideal and its effectiveness as a standard of measurement regarding the behavior of others:

Not that it is always necessary to accede to wishes or desires of others, to hold or keep their respect, love, hope or faith. But know in *whom* as well as in what you believe! And if thy faith is founded in the spiritual, the Creative, the constructive forces, it brings peace and harmony.

Then let thy heart, thy mind, determine within itself. See and be in that attitude as given of old; letting others do as they will or may, but for thee ye will cleave to a *living* God, a *living* hope, a *living* faith—an *activative* experience!

Thus, as ye do this, the other things may pass. 1189-2

The emphasis here is on God as a living, animate being, not merely a mental concept. The reading continues by offering various physical and psychospiritual therapeutics. It advises treatments with hydrotherapy and electrotherapy, followed by a change of environment. It also warns against the use of any medications:

As you find, there has been created an inactivative force—other than repellent—between the sympathetic nervous system and the judgments; or the cerebrospinal nerve reaction of positive fact or nature. Hence as we will find, change of scene and of environment will be well. But *first* we would have the low electrical forces that would *attune* the bodily forces to coordinate one with another. Then also we would have the hydrotherapy and the electrical forces.

Do not resort to drug of *any* nature. For upon same as to bring those appetites that would become—the vibrations of the mental and spiritual will only rebel, or so feed upon same as to bring those appetites that would become—to the mental and spiritual forces of the entity—repellent in their end. 1189-2

Next, the individual is advised to develop habit patterns based on service to others. Notice how the reading redirects her natural tendency to "keep busy" toward more constructive ends. It also recommends that she keep a schedule of her activities:

> Work and associate with those influences or forces wherein there is help being lent or given to others. This will also create an atmosphere, and attitude for the body mentally and physically that will be constructive. For the very nature of the entity, and of the impelling influences that we have indicated for the body, is to be *busy!*
>
> Then let it be a *constructive* forces, but keep busy—no matter in what direction, keep busy! As we find, these adhered to will bring about the better reactions. At first it may appear that these are not very definite, but let the body make out a schedule for itself in this manner . . . 1189-2

The first part of the "schedule" focuses on working with ideals:

> So much time each day *(and do it!)* I will give to the improvement of my mental concept of my relationships to Creative Forces of God. 1189-2

The next part of the schedule is to include periods of relaxation alternating with exercise. This serves to harmonize the mind with the body for the better expression of her ideals:

> So much time each day I will give to *physical* relaxation and exertion for expression, for the activities to produce the proper coordinant relationships between mind and the body. 1189-2

Finally, the schedule is to incorporate times when these ideals are expressed on a daily basis through her attitudes and behavior:

> "So much time I will give *(and give it!)*, each day, to putting into *practice* that which is *perceived* and *conceived*, as to thy relationships to the Creative Forces, thy relationships to thy fellow man." And not necessarily those in high places, nor altogether those who have lost hope. For the body, mind and soul needs the encouragements as well as the concrete forces of example where hope has been and is lost, that must be revived by thy activity. 1189-2

This reading can serve as a basic model for the Cayce viewpoint on depression. In all cases, as in this one, causes are multifaceted, and treatment is holistic. Physical therapeutics include osteopathy, physiotherapy, electrotherapy, diet, exercise, and others. These become more specific as physical pathology is present in the overall condition. Psychospiritual therapeutics are based on the need to establish a spiritual foundation for one's existence. This is accomplished by establishing spiritual, mental, and physical ideals and forming new habit patterns based on them. These are to replace old patterns grounded in ego and personality. In setting ideals, the readings encourage individuals to have only the highest aspirations for themselves. One man is told that his ideal:

> . . . has not been set high enough. Remember, when standards or ideals are measured by human activities, these are only of finite minds, and are not viewed except through the eyes of the beholder; and since these are only of mental or of moral is-

sues as well, these must be set as high as the heavens themselves . . . 5489-1

As we have seen, the highest standard recommended in the readings is that of the Christ. This is emphasized again and again:

> Q. *How can I rise above my last period of depression and feel that I am going forward again?*
> A. Set thine thoughts and thine mind on things that pertain to His love, His will, and those things that would hinder become as the shadows in the background, and look not upon that in the rear—rather pressing on to the mark of high calling as set in Him that has been put in thine *own* ideal, in the Christ life, the Christ Consciousness; for in Him *is* hope, life, peace, harmony, understanding. 288-30

Once the spiritual ideal is established, the readings encourage its expression on both a psychological and behavioral level, by replacing destructive habit patterns with more constructive ones. Let's now look at their psychospiritual recommendations alongside those from today's psychology.

The readings tell us that one way of handling depression is to work with behavior. They repeatedly encourage one to challenge destructive behavior patterns of self-condemnation, resentment, regret, discouragement, remorse, self-pity, jealousy, fault-finding, hate, impatience, and many others. The following excerpt reflects a theme seen in many readings:

> *Do not* condemn others! *Do not* condemn *self!* Self-condemnation for that which is past, that which cannot be rectified, is but to heap reproach upon self. Reproach not self *nor* others . . . 5469-1

Destructive patterns are to be replaced with more positive, constructive ones based in selflessness and reflecting one's spiritual ideal. The formation of these patterns can be facilitated by associating positive reinforcement with new behaviors. You could, for example, make a specific effort to praise someone, be friendly or kind to someone, and so on. Following this action, you would reward yourself in some way, so that the new behavior stays with you. What the reward is will depend on what you like. It could be a special dessert, going fishing, playing golf, anticipating social approval, a sense of pride, and a host of other things. Rewards are more effective when they are made contingent with the new behavior. The readings add to this by promising additional rewards, based on karmic laws. Such rewards would serve as additional positive reinforcers, strengthening the new behavior pattern even more. This is evident in the following:

Know that with what measure you mete it is measured to you. If you would have friends, be friendly. If you would even have fun, make fun for someone else. 3440-2

Working with behavior can also involve environmental manipulations or stimulus control. The readings on depression often recommend putting oneself in certain situations to facilitate the development of certain patterns. One way to do this is through exposure to philosophical and inspirational literature, or bibliotherapy. A woman is advised to study:

. . . some form of philosophy as to the relationships of individuals to those environs about them; that is, these should be the basis of such study—not cisms or cults, not those things that are intended to form merely attitudes or cliques or classes or the like, but rather those things that are based upon the commandments—especially those recommendations of Moses in his last admonition.

Here (that is, in those chapters) we will find that which is both of the mental and the spiritual, as related to not only the relationships of individual entities to their fellow men but also their relationships to Creative Forces or God. 2325-1

In this excerpt, the individual is directed to study literature that focuses on ideals, rather than ideas. Ideas relate to ego and, as such, are represented by various "cisms," "cults," "cliques," and "classes." Ideals, on the other hand, are absolute in essence and reflect the Big I and individuality. They are found in "those things that are based upon the commandments." The challenge in this reading is the formation of new patterns based in ideals. Biblical references for depression were often similar to those for anxiety. Individuals were directed to both the Old and New Testaments: One person is told to:

See, feel, use the promises that are thine from the study especially of the 14th, 15th, 16th and 17th of John. Let them be as words to *thee!* 1614-1

Notice here again how the reading emphasizes the personal message inherent in the biblical passage. In addition to bibliotherapy, the readings often recommend stimulus control through other environmental changes. This can be seen in the following comments:

. . . such an environment is needed in a more open surrounding, or at home, or at some quiet place where there can be a great deal of compan-

ionship, of study, of reasoning, yes of spiritual reasoning together. 3662-1

. . . the body needs rest, with body, mind, and
with little to do but plenty of those surroundings
well pleasing to the body. 49-1

We can appreciate here the specifics of the environmental recommendations. If you use this technique,
you'll have to decide what type of situation is best suited
for your particular development. In addition to using
these behavioral strategies in working with depression,
you can also reconcile the Cayce recommendations with
the other ones we discussed. Another solution recommended in the readings is the use of reason to challenge
irrational beliefs and cognitive distortions. One belief
that is common to depression is the idea that one is helpless and hopeless and has no control over the situation.
The comeback here is to see that control does exist, to
the extent that one maintains rational thought patterns.
The readings not only agree with this, but emphasize
free will as the defining characteristic of the individual.
At the level of personality this means that one is neither
hopeless nor helpless but can alter events in life. The key
is to choose the correct form of action. This is evident in
the answer given to the following question:

Q. Were evil forces warring within me or was it my
reasoning mind that caused this depression?
A. As has been given from the beginning, "There
is set before thee good and evil. Choose thou." In
the choosing, in the setting of thine will in that direction or the other direction allows those influences to become magnified or lessened by that in
the promises. 288-30

Thought restructuring can also be employed to challenge personalization, a cognitive distortion often seen in depression. Here, the individual assumes responsibility for everything that happens in life, leading to many guilt feelings. The argument against this is understanding that each of us is responsible for his or her own actions and underscoring this with the primacy of free will in human affairs. As one's life is an interplay of will with karma, each is in a situation that is self-created and self-reflective. Each one is responsible, whether the situation is good or bad, whether it entails pleasure or suffering. So long as the action of free will is guided by selflessness, there is no reason for guilt.

The readings also recommend the use of imagination to combat depression. As we have seen, this can be done in several ways. For instance, you can employ covert modeling as a way of identifying with your Big I and its ideal expression. One way to do this is by personifying the Big I in some manner and using it as a role model. If you were to use Jesus here, you could try to imagine how He would respond to a particular situation associated with your depression. You would imagine all aspects of Him, including verbal expressions, facial expressions, body language, and so on. As you picture His behavior in your mind, you would attempt to merge with it, seeing yourself doing the same things. The following reading recommends such an identification and tells the individual to:

> . . . find that the voice is speaking from within and directing to self what the self may do in its relationships to others. Make these a portion of self and of self's attitudes towards others. 770-1

You can also use positive visualization to create new attitudes and behavior patterns. One individual is told:

The abilities for the imaginative experiences, the imaginative influences, those having to do with relationships with others, have been and are an *enormous* experience through which the entity has lost sight, or failed to see the possibilities of, in the present application. 2160-1

In using positive visualization, you would construct a mental movie where you see yourself engaging in some form of altruistic behavior. You could, for example, imagine someone else who is depressed and see yourself comforting him, giving him courage, making him laugh, and other constructive behaviors. Your scenario would be as detailed as possible, and focus on only the positive. Such an approach can be especially helpful when your symptoms of depression include a loss of motivation and interest in life. Still another way of working with the power of imagination is with hypnosis. This was recommended in the readings on several occasions. In one case, an individual is given advice for the:

. . . subjugation through those of a subliminal nature, to reach that inner self through the suggestion, see? As suggestion is to the mind, the builder, then we will find, by the subjugation of the own personnel [personal], or personality in the present condition, we would bring that, through proper suggestion, which would build in a normal manner. 186-2

One of the safest ways to use suggestion is during the hypnagogic state. As the readings place the roots of habits in the subconscious mind, one of the easiest ways to approach them is during pre-sleep. To do this, you could make up positive, constructive affirmations that you would repeat to yourself as you fall asleep. For example, if your self-esteem is low, the affirmation might be, "As a child of God, I am unique and special." If your depression relates to interpersonal problems, the affirmation might be, "I am a friendly person," "I am a kind person," and statements of this nature. If you suffer from guilt feelings, you might say, "I behave in a selfless and helpful manner." In using pre-sleep suggestions, make the affirmation short. Simply repeat it to yourself as you drift off into sleep, or use a tape recorder to help you. In addition to the use of these imaginative strategies, the other ones we mentioned can also be readily reconciled with the readings. The Cayce materials also include additional psychospiritual strategies that revolve around interests, hobbies, careers, and many other areas. One individual, who had communistic tendencies, is told:

> Hence in the present, any of that activity in which there is social service, or a philanthropic activity for the betterment of those underprivileged individuals, will be a channel through which the entity may find the greater outlet for its abilities. However, this will necessitate that the entity keep self from being too much in the communistic trend. While the ideas of a communistic nature are well, as indicated, they are not *ideal* when expressed or manifested in relationships to *real* social service. For, such activities should arise by and through the promptings of the spiritual, rather than wholly the material gains from same. 1614-2

The variety of psychospiritual recommendations of the readings, complemented with techniques from today's psychology, can be quite effective in coping with depression. As we saw with the anxiety disorders, the readings repeatedly integrate them with prayer and meditation. The significance of these practices cannot be underestimated. Look at how one reading answers a most serious question:

Q. *Why is the thought always with me to kill myself?*

A. Self-condemnation. For, not enough of that seeking to manifest God's will has been manifested. When this thought occurs, let thy prayer be as indicated: *"Lord, here am I—Thine! Use me in those ways and manners as Thou seest, that I may ever glorify Thee."* 2540-1

In the next case, the importance of meditation is discussed:

Give not away to the satisfying of thine own indulgences and say, "What's the use; no one cares!" If thou dost not care for thyself, who may care for thee? . . . And look to that from within. For He, thy God, thy better self, thy inner man, thy Christ Consciousness, thine own soul, hath promised to meet thee there—and to guide thee in all things that will make for making thine experience in the earth not only a joyous one but more and more worthwhile for those that thou dost contact day by day. And thy light, thy word, shall *shine*—if ye will but enter in! 802-2

Notice here how the ideal of the Christ is also referred to as "God," "better self," "inner man," and "thine own soul." As we saw earlier, it is the Christ pattern that represents the perfect actualization of individuality. It is imprinted in each of us and is awakened with meditation. In working with the readings on depression, remember once again the importance of writing things down. Look over your problem analysis list, your target symptoms, and your goals. Select a strategy that fits your personality style and indicate everything in a contract. As you begin to tackle your depression, remember the importance of consistency, persistence, and, above all, patience.

13

Alcohol Dependence: Drinking That Is Out of Control

Q. Is the moderate use of alcohol injurious to this body and what is moderate for this body?
A. Occasionally if you took a drink—once a year, it wouldn't be too bad—but wouldn't be too good either. Not that one becomes a total abstainer . . . when in Rome, do as the Romans, but needn't get drunk over it, nor become so that ye seek too much of those things!

Edgar Cayce reading 416-18

Alcoholism is a disorder that affects many people. It is a common problem that sometimes occurs alone and often accompanies other psychological disorders. It can have devastating effects on one's life, including physical problems, family discord, and work-related difficulties, just to name a few. While most people have common-sense notions about alcoholism, the DSM-IV[1] lists specific criteria for different types of alcohol-related disorders. The most frequent of these is *alcohol dependence.* Here, the use of alcohol results in distress or functional impairment as expressed in at least three symptoms at any time over a period of one year. One symptom is tolerance. When you tolerate something, it means you get used to it. Alcohol tolerance means that the body gets used to drinking, and as a result, the amount one drinks becomes ineffective. This could lead to a need for more alcohol to experience its effects. Another symptom is withdrawal. This refers to certain effects that follow the cessation of heavy drinking, such as nausea, sweating, hand tremors, agitation, hallucinations, seizures, and others. It also refers to the ingestion of alcohol to avoid such problems or to relieve them once they occur. In addition to tolerance and withdrawal, the alcohol dependent person may drink more than intended or for longer periods of time. Attempts to cut down drinking are unsuccessful, despite one's efforts. A great deal of time revolves around alcohol, such as in obtaining it, using it, or dealing with its effects. The alcohol dependent person may give up important areas of life as a result of drinking, such as work, recreation, and social activities. Finally, the individual may continue to drink despite its contributory role in specific physical or psychological problems, as, for example, heart disease. Remember, alcohol dependence means having three or more of these symptoms any time over a period of one year.

Like all problems in life, the Cayce readings see alcohol dependence as having its primary origin in an existential crisis of separation where the Big I diverted from the divine pattern in its expression. This repeated itself on all levels of consciousness, where each phase of development was affected by every other phase. The present drinking problem reflects an attempt of the soul to understand the error of its ways. In some cases, the readings show a past-life connection to present drinking patterns. This can be seen in the following comments:

Before that we find the entity was in the environs and activities of the Roman land, where there were those disturbances wrought by the activities of the peoples between that we know in the present as church and state—or when there were the attempts of those in authority to direct the abilities or activities of those who would worship in a given direction according to the dictates of their own conscience.

Thus we find the entity, in the name of Calper [?], was one of the guards that through duty brought destruction and death to those who followed in a way in which there were those choices to be made as to whether they would be torn asunder or deny the moving, motivative forces of their lives.

There we find the entity was torn within self, and yet declaring the sense of duty. Hence oft there was the necessity for subjugating the body through either alcohol or other influences to cause the body to forget.

Thus the entity became one subjugated to the appetites of satisfying the bodily needs—in the attempt to forget. 1969-2

Here we see a remote cause relating the use of alcohol in one lifetime where it functioned to block out distressing events. In another case, a woman is told how she and her husband had abused alcohol during a Grecian incarnation and should not repeat this in the present:

Thus it has been and is the problem of each in the present to prevent the satisfying, the gratifying of *bodily* influence or emotions which arise for the moment—or appetites, or influences. 934-7

An interesting case is a reading given for a fourteen-year-old girl at the request of her mother. It warns of potential drinking and eating problems she could develop by being exposed to a drinking environment.

> There will be these as warnings, these for those responsible for the entity: A tendency for the body to overeat or to be overindulgent in appetites. Be warned for self, as well as associates of those who take wine or strong drink, for this may easily become a stumbling block to the entity. 5359-1

The warning here is given to "those responsible" for the girl. The cause of this tendency is traced back to a previous lifetime following the American Revolution. Look at the interesting connection:

> Here we find the entity interested in building a home with the beautiful grounds about same.
> In the name then Lila Chapman, the entity gained through the period, for the home to the entity and its family, and its children was that which took the greater portion of its time, save the study of the Word which was given place in that home; and yet there came from same those who took too much of the cup, as cheers. This brought disturbances, sorrows. Don't let it occur again. There will be the tendencies for attraction, not only for self, but for those about you. For that ye hate has come upon thee. Don't hate anything in the present. 5359-1

It appears that during that lifetime, the individual was distressed by the drinking that was taking place and expressed it through a pattern of hostility. Her present lifetime represents a corrective reaction to this. In addition to past-life influences, the effects of astrological so-

journs were also evident in problems of alcohol dependence, as seen in the following comments:

> . . . in this entity [we have] one that may be taken
> from the earth's plane of understanding . . . as an
> ensample of conditions as may be wrought with will
> exercised in the right and in the wrong manner, and
> the influences of astrological conditions as exer-
> cised in the earth's plane. 304-5

Here we can also see a very important concern the
readings have about drinking; namely, its potentially
destructive effect on one's will. This is a matter that we'll
consider more fully below. Pre-life experiences create
patterns which interact with that of the physical body at
birth. If these patterns are associated with prior alcohol-
related situations, they can predispose the individual to
alcohol dependence at any point in life. In one case, a
woman with a drinking problem is advised to watch the
development of her newborn son:

> For, it will be found that the greater temptation
> to the offspring will be imbibing too freely of the
> cup! 934-7

Predispositions to alcohol dependence can be centered in spiritual, mental, or physical factors. Since these
are interdependent, such propensities usually reflect a
system in conflict. All predispositions interact with various events occurring in life, as well as with the action of
one's will. The most significant of these events is drinking itself. Many individuals asked Cayce if drinking was
harmful to them. Although his answers were tailor-made
for each person, the usual response called for modera-
tion. He also noted the beneficial effects of light wines in
combination with certain foods. The readings empha-

sized, however, that excessive drinking of any alcoholic beverage can lead to serious problems. One person who asks about the effects of whiskey on health and longevity is told:

> . . . you are suffering from the use of some of these in the present; but it is overindulgence. In moderation these are not too bad, but man so seldom will be moderate. Or, as most say, those who even indulge will make themselves pigs, but we naturally are pigs when there is overindulgence. This, of course, makes for conditions which are to be met. For what one sows that must one reap. This is [an] unchangeable law. 5233-1

The "overindulgence" in alcohol is one of the most significant immediate causes of alcohol dependence. A potentially dangerous situation especially arises when drinking is used as a coping mechanism for stress. Many individuals requesting readings had stress-related problems and found quick relief in alcohol. The danger lies in the fact that alcohol affects the total, interactive system of body, mind, and spirit, so that predispositions toward alcohol dependence as well as other life experiences in this direction can bring it out. These other experiences can at first be totally unrelated to the problem but can plant the seeds for its occurrence. In several readings Cayce noted the relationship between drinking problems and earlier accidents and injuries. One man was given two readings. In the first he is told:

> Now as we find, from the physical disturbances these, while they appear to be minor, are deep-seated and come from pressures between the coordinating of the sensory forces and the activities of the deeper organs.

Thus we have periods when there are greater disturbances that find their reaction in gratifying of appetites. 1439-1

When asked in the second reading about the origin of these deep-seated "pressures," Cayce responds:

Pressure between moving machinery of some kind—cars. 1439-2

This shows us that the individual's drinking adversely affected an already dysfunctional physiology due to a previous injury. In another case, strain was implicated as a causative factor. This individual is told:

In the 6th and 7th dorsal center we find a subluxation that was caused sometime back, by an outside influence or strain to that area, which caused an excess flow of conditions in the form of nerve impulse to the digestive system, that calls for appetite satisfaction. 2161-1

Other readings talked about the contribution of general mental attitudes to alcohol dependence. In the next excerpt, the interaction of these with a physical disturbance is mentioned:

Q. *What was the original cause, or what brought about this condition?*
A. Changes in the glandular system, and then aggravated by animosities and hate. 3315-1

Other readings showed how drinking related to previous medical conditions. In one case, a man was suffering from neuritis, and to deal with the pain, he apparently used both sedatives and alcohol. This, however, only made a bad situation worse, as it exacerbated his desire to drink. His drinking became more excessive as a result of some financial problems he incurred. It is at this point where his wife requested a reading from Cayce. In her letter she writes:

> "Nearly eighteen months ago we moved to my mother's home to live and [486] said the reason was because of financial losses, but after being there a short while we found that he was drinking very heavily. I have no idea when he started but he says he did a little while before we moved when he began to lose so much by the farmers in the insurance business." 486-1 Reports

The reading discusses the complications resulting from his previous maladaptive attempts to cope with the pain of neuritis. This condition, in turn, is traced back to:

> . . . a prolapsus in the colon area. This is from a strain in the early portion of the life that, had it been brought to normalcy when the body was developing—or when those conditions were in a position before the system had adjusted itself, would have been easy. 486-1

As with any psychological disorder, this case highlights the complexities of etiological factors. If we look for immediate causes beyond karmic propensities present at birth, we can see how an original "strain" initiated the problem. This proliferated into alcohol dependence over a period of years and incorporated other factors including neuritis, financial problems, and, especially, maladaptive coping strategies in the misapplication of free will by excessive drinking. Some readings discussed the spiritual ramifications of drinking, indicating that excesses in this area represented divergences from the ideals inherent in one's individuality. This can be seen in Cayce's answer to the question:

> Q. *Are the use of tobacco and alcohol harmful to my physical condition?*
> A. What is your ideal? Would you prepare these for that you would worship as your Maker? If you would, use them. If you wouldn't, they are harmful. 3100-1

Since excessive drinking satisfies ego interests, it reinforces the separateness of personality away from the ideals of the Big I. The psychological reaction to this often appears as guilt and remorse. These feelings, in turn, lead to denial, a common defense mechanism in alcohol dependence. Here, the person refuses to acknowledge the problem.

While the interaction of spiritual, mental, and physical causes must be addressed in the etiology of alcohol dependence, the readings make a very interesting point about the potential role of physical factors. It is well known that there is a physiological reaction to the ingestion of alcohol. In excessive amounts and taken over long periods of time, it results in damage. This is evident in the fact that a great number of people in hospitals are suffering from alcohol-related problems. The readings explain how physiological damage occurs and its subsequent mediating role in future drinking patterns. They tell us that drinking alters the body in such a way that the very desire to drink intensifies. This means that what can start out as a seemingly innocuous way of dealing with stress can result in a most tenacious habit. It is at this point where alcohol dependence becomes a physical addiction or disease.

The readings thus agree with two conflicting, contemporary views of alcohol dependence. One says that drinking is a psychological condition and the other that it is a physical disease. According to Cayce, both notions are correct, depending on what level the body becomes affected. Early drinking patterns result in minor biological adjustments. With continued, excessive drinking, however, these become major incoordinations in the body, resulting in physical damage that exacerbates the desire. We saw this in the above example of the individual suffering from neuritis, and it is a common theme in many readings. One man is told:

> Now as we find, there are disturbances. Some . . . in special reference to the desire for drink, are the aftereffects of the indulgence in same, and the effect upon the nervous system as well as the liver, the pancreas, the spleen and the kidneys. 2010-1

Notice here how the urge to drink relates to the "aftereffects" of prior drinking patterns. The next cases show the same thing happening and also point out the complexity of the problem:

> Now, as we find, there are definite disturbances in the physical forces of the body that make for those reactions that produce the incontrollable appetites, and the activities of the body in those directions where there is the tendency for the body to produce or make for—within self— condemnations that make for those activities that only aggravate, or produce the greater tendencies for those physical conditions that are disturbed to *magnify* in the body the desires. 606-1

This individual suffered a nervous breakdown resulting from financial losses. What probably began as drinking to reduce stress, caused significant bodily damage that exacerbated his desire into "incontrollable appetites." This, in turn, led to more drinking, as well as to self-deprecation, resulting in further biological deterioration and the magnification of his craving. It is interesting to note in this case how the body is affected, not only by the pattern of drinking but also by the attitude that is held. The physical role in alcohol dependence was also understood by the waking Cayce as he examined the readings he gave. In a letter to one individual, he writes:

"From the reading, evidently habit creates a condition in the physical system, much like—if you will pardon the expression—a hog finding a gap in the fence. It may be a good fence in every way except the gap." 1427-1 Reports

The "gap," of course, refers to the physiological disturbance created by alcohol consumption. How do physiological factors actually exacerbate the desire to drink? This is answered in the next case where the person suffered an injury resulting in a nervous system incoordination. As the reading shows, this was adversely affected by his drinking:

Activities to the sensory system—eyes, ears, nose, throat and activities here—are overexaggerated; so that at times just by the mere odor of this or that the appetites are enlivened to such states, such conditions, that these become intolerable to the body. At other times the sight of various activities or conditions bring to bear on the mind those impulses that, receiving that incoordination between the cerebrospinal and sympathetic system, become overactive to portions of the body. Hence these

must be as impulses, as appetites, as any condition
wherein there is what may be termed the forming
of habits . . . 606-1

Here we can see the sensitivity of the individual to
various alcohol-related sensory cues relative to the incoordination of his nervous system, especially to odors
and visual stimuli. One way to understand this is to recall a time when you were very hungry, when you hadn't
eaten for a long time. How did you react when you sat
down to eat? Didn't the food look, smell, and taste better
than usual? What happens here is that the intensity of
the hunger drive makes you more sensitive to food-re-
lated stimuli, so that the food has a more positive effect.
This occurs even if you eat something that you normally
dislike.

Something similar happens in alcohol dependence
when its habitual nature incorporates physical factors.
As the above reading puts it, stimulation to the sensory
systems of the body become "overexaggerated. This
means that the threshold for excitation and positive feelings related to alcoholic beverages is lowered significantly, so that a drink, or anything associated with it, is
attractive and alluring. Once physiological factors play a
contributory role in alcohol dependence, a major concern becomes the undermining of free will. One individual is told:

> . . . there *are* evidences of a weakness in the
> *physical* body through the desire for *gratifying* of
> appetite that has blocked the will of the mental
> forces by gratifying of a physical desire for the emo-
> tions of a mental and physical experience; thus be-
> coming a destructive influence to the physical and
> the mental body. 1427-1

The weakening of will is linked to physical pathology:

Then, how have these activities so worked, so manifested themselves upon the physical as to deplete that resistance which should manifest itself in a physically, materially, *well* body?

In the gratifying of a desire, these become habit-forming; in the manner of the effect then of the drug and the effects of alcohol upon the system weakening the will and thus weakening the coordination between the manifestation of spiritual truth with material gratification of flesh desires.

These we find manifest themselves upon the nervous system of the body, and give expressions in the nerve system between the cerebrospinal *and* the vegetative or sympathetic nerve system.

Hence from the continual gratifying of an emotion or desire for those things that dull or subdue, or put aside the effects of a mental reaction, we find that physically there are pressures that exist in the ganglia of the upper dorsal and through the cervical areas, that magnify then the desire for gratifying upon the cardiac and the second cardiac system.

Thus the craving, the gnawing in the gastric forces of the digestive system—or the liver and heart activity in its ganglia—makes for the *inordinate desire!*

So the body becomes physically overcome by the mental anguish produces by *desire* upon the system.

Hence we find not only are there the effects of the desire but these are magnified by associations, by environs; and there is then—in the nervous system, through those pressures and in those areas indicated—the longing for gratification. 1427-1

We can see here the complex interplay of factors contributing to the habit pattern of alcohol dependence. Further, we can appreciate its negative impact on will as it weakens "the coordination between the manifestation of spiritual truth with material gratification of flesh desires." This means that as alcohol dependence weakens the will, it prevents the channeling of one's spiritual essence.

The worst-case scenario is possession. Here, the physiological condition deteriorates to the point that the person is susceptible to "outside" influences. This refers to discarnate beings that can "attach" themselves to such individuals. While the idea of possession is foreign to the majority of psychological theories, the multidimensional worldview of the readings allows for effects of this kind. They tell us that it is not an unusual occurrence in cases of alcohol dependence, as well as in other psychological disorders, especially the psychoses. Look at the way Cayce answers a woman's question about her husband's drinking problem:

> Q. *Regarding my husband, what is meant by "possession"?*
> A. Means *possession!*
> Q. *Does that mean by other entities, while under the influence of liquor?*
> A. By others while under the influence that causes those reactions and makes for the antagonism, and the very *change* of the activities. 1183-3

In another case, a man is told in a reading:

> Here we find that we have both a pathological and a psychological effect; or we have those tendencies such that—from a pathological condition—influences outside the body oft affect the

sympathetic or suggestive or psychic self. 3432-1

The "influences outside the body" refer to discarnates. This is again evident in the next case:

> Not a possession, save when there begins the gratifying of same; *then* there are the opportunities for those influences from without to possess the activities of the body in not only the cunningness of the activities but in that which to the *body*, under the influence, becomes as reasonableness to the influences and activities of that possession. 1439-1

Notice here how the "influences" are assimilated into the personality of the individual and foster his denial, allowing him to impute "reasonableness" into his maladaptive lifestyle. In an earlier reading for herself, the wife of this man asked Cayce if her husband's craving for alcohol was an organic condition or possession. Cayce gives her an interesting answer:

> An organic disturbance is merely a possession when it has reached the nth degree as to be possession. 845-4

This tells us that possession occurs once an individual's physical pathology reaches a critical level.

As we can see, the causes of alcohol dependence, like the other psychological disorders, are complex. The readings address a system in conflict, comprising spiritual, mental, and physical components. Once again, the treatment recommendations are holistic and are geared to bringing this system into harmony. Emphasis is placed on physical therapeutics as the problem reaches the stage of physical addiction or disease. These include

chemical intervention, osteopathy, massage, hydrotherapy, electrotherapy, diet, and others. Psychospiritual
therapeutics are nonspecific, emphasizing the need to
establish a spiritual foundation in one's existence and to
live by it.

The following reading will be presented in its entirety
and can serve as a model enabling you to appreciate the
complexity of this problem, as well as to understand the
rationale of the treatment recommendations. It was
given for a twenty-six-year-old man, based on a request
from his father. The reading begins as follows:

> As we find, while there are physical disturbances
> with this body, these arise as much from the mental
> attitudes—that were in the beginning taken as
> poses, and have grown to become rather conditions
> that are of the *self;* or as habits, as requirements,
> that have taken on those aspects from the *mental*
> standpoint that are *almost*—or at times, and under
> or in certain environments, become—*possessions!*
> 1106-1

As can be seen, the problem began in the mind as
"poses." While it is not clear what exactly was meant by
this, we may assume that the individual initially drank
for a certain effect. This pattern developed into a habit,
once physiological damage occurred, and produced tendencies toward possession. The reading continues:

> For in its final analysis, in the physical and men-
> tal activities of a body, it—the body—*mentally*—is
> continually meeting itself and that it (the body,
> mentally) had done about *constructive* or creative
> forces within the body itself. 1106-1

This passage pointed to the karmic nature of the problem. The individual was told that he was presently confronting his previous errors or the misapplication of "creative forces." Next, therapeutic recommendations are given:

> Then, as we find, to meet the needs of the conditions in this body, it must—or will—require that which will enable the body to either *become* determined within itself to *meet* its own self in *spiritual* reaction, or such a change of environment that will require the mental and physical reactions of the body to be such as to *enable* it (the body, mentally *and* physically) to *induce* that within the physical reactions to take possession in the place of, or to replace, those habit-forming conditions in the mental, as to rid the body of these conditions. 1106-1

Here, the individual was given two strategies to consider in replacing his destructive drinking habit. The first involved a determination and a strong act of will to help himself, by harmonizing his personality with his individuality. The second was a "change of environment," or institutionalization. This is similar to what is referred today as detox. The reading continues with psycho-spiritual recommendations:

> These, as we find, then, will *aid* in doing this:
> Let the environs, in the first, be whereunto that the body will make a study of that which *is* expressed or shown in the reading (not only reading but the *feeling as* reading) of the twelfth chapter in Romans, and then the 14th, 15th, 16th and 17th [fourteenth, fifteenth, sixteenth and seventeenth] chapters of John. 1106-1

The twelfth chapter in Romans speaks of the interrelationship of all human beings in Christ and the contributions each makes in life. It also deals with fraternal charity, or doing good deeds. As we saw earlier, the passages from John show how Jesus actualized the divine pattern in the Christ and how all individualities revolve around this pattern. Like his approach to all psychological disorders, Cayce is showing this individual the need to establish a spiritual foundation in his life. The reading continues by suggesting physical therapeutics to enable him to build up his will:

> And during such periods, or throughout such periods of study, we would take internally a combination of Chloride of Gold and Bromide of Soda. Prepare the two solutions and keep separate, in this manner; in these proportions:
> Add one (1) grain of Chloride of Gold to (1) ounce of distilled water. This would be one solution.
> Add three (3) grains of Bromide of Soda to one (1) ounce of distilled water. This would be the other solution.
> When taken (which would preferably be of a morning before the meal is eaten), the dosage would be: 1st day: One (1) minim (or drop) of the Gold solution and two (2) minims (drops) of the Soda solution, in half a glass of water. 2nd day: Two (2) minims of the Gold solution and 4 minims of the Soda solution. 3rd day: Three (3) minims of the Gold solution and 6 minims of the Soda solution.
> Then leave off for three days. Then begin again. Continue in this manner. 1106-1

Cayce's "Gold Cure" was a common recommendation for the treatment of alcohol dependence. What it did was to build up the person's resistance to drinking by inducing a negative reaction to it. This is most interesting, as it is a prototype of aversion therapy, a common form of treatment used today in treating drinking problems. As the reading continues, the individual is told:

> This will, as we find, *aid* the body *physically* to *respond mentally* to the impressionable forces that are made upon the body through the reading of those texts or portions of writing indicated. 1106-1

In other words, by building up his body's resistance to the craving for alcohol, the individual could facilitate his spiritual attunement as he studied the suggested biblical passages. He is told, however, that while the physical treatment was necessary, it was not sufficient and success would ultimately be based on his determination:

> If this is done, we will find there *can* be the response—provided the body will *determine* it within itself.
> Do this for a period of thirty-six days, and we will give further instructions. 1106-1

Next, he is told:

> In the diet, let it be regular. 1106-1

The reading ends by encouraging the individual to strengthen his will and to determine to change his behavior through the application of spiritual truths:

> Let the body keep the surroundings such that will be in keeping with those things that are *determined* within self; to be good *for* something, that there may be the expression of the spirit that is inter-

preted in the body being the temple of the living God—and hence should, by all right, be kept holy, inviolate, and presented as a living sacrifice, holy, acceptable unto Him.

Then know and realize the truth of those words set forth in the prayer, the meditation of the Master; "Lo, I am with thee always—be *not* afraid; trust in me, for in my Father's house are the mansions." Within thine own self are the abilities to meet, to do, to accomplish. *Do* it! 1106-1

As can be seen, the individual is advised to put mental and physical ideals into practice, or to "be good *for* something." He is told to find comfort in the words of Jesus. Such a course of action would not only effect symptom relief but, more important, spiritual awakening. While this case can be taken as a model, it is important to keep in mind that Cayce responded to individual needs of the soul. Information given for all psychological problems was geared to the unique situation in life encountered by each person requesting a reading. While generalities are evident throughout the readings, the specifics have to be appreciated. This is evident in the following comments:

> Q. *In alcoholic cases, can a general outline of treatment be given?*
> A. No. Each individual has its own individual problems. Not *all* are *physical.* Hence there are those that are of the sympathetic nature, or where there has been the possession by the very activity of same . . . 606-1

Generalities, of course, are based on spiritual ideals or the need to establish a spiritual foundation for existence. As told to one individual, the reason for this is:

. . . so that the spiritual promises may be put to active service and work to replace the habits with the habits of doing *good*, doing right, doing justice, being merciful. 1427-1

Let us now turn to the psychospiritual recommendations of the readings and coordinate them with psychological strategies. It is important to remember that, among the various destructive effects of alcohol dependence, the depletion of will is of special concern in the readings. This, of course, relates to the importance ascribed to free will in human nature. Their recommendations, therefore, often revolve around strengthening the will. While Cayce advised abstinence and determination as a way of doing this, he was aware of its limitations due to the complexities underlying the disorder, especially once physical factors became more salient. The psychospiritual recommendations for alcohol dependence employ the use of imagination, reason, and behavior, sometimes alone, more often in combination. For instance, Cayce usually suggested bibliotherapy. While he was apparently aware of the twelve-step program of Alcoholics Anonymous, he did not refer to it. Instead, he turned to the Bible, advising that certain passages be read. Moreover, as we have seen, he encouraged the person to identity with it, to see that it was written personally for him or her. At times, bibliotherapy was recommended for simultaneous use with imagination and physical therapeutics, as seen here:

Study these passages at periods when ye have a Radio-Active Appliance tied to you. Read them. Then close thine eyes and visualize it working within thy mind and body. You'll be proud of those about you and of yourself. 3432-1

This can be viewed as the use of positive visualization to form more constructive patterns by coordinating spirit, mind, and body. The same was evident in the next case. Here, bibliotherapy is not suggested, but instead the individual is encouraged to focus on constructive attitudes while using the Wet Cell Appliance to assist him in this direction:

Then let the mental attitudes of the body—during the periods when the applications of the vibrations are used from the Appliance—turn to that of *seeing*, within self, what is to be, what *may* be, and what *is being* accomplished by such applications in the body-physical; if the directions of the mental self are in that direction.

For as the impulses of the nervous system, through the mental attitudes, are directed in a constructive influence and force, we will find the conditions improving; and the abilities of the mental self to keep in more constructive attitudes . . . For the strength of Creative Forces and Energies will and does build constructively in the body, if the attitudes and activities are coordinated. 1439-2

The use of imagination through hypnosis was also recommended as a helpful technique. One individual is told:

. . . there may be applied the suggestive forces in putting the consciousness into that position where the awareness of the subconscious force may become a part of the consciousness, and thus maintain a better equilibrium of the flow of activity of the impulses to the supersensitive forces of the body-force itself; bringing then, through such subjugation, the awareness of itself, its condition, its needs and its desires. 1969-2

In the next case, hypnosis was recommended as an alternative to hospitalization. Notice here the emphasis put on the need for the individual to sustain his will:

> Either, then, through applications of subjugating the conscious mind through hypnosis or through those treatments that may be accorded in those places where both drink *and* sedatives may be taken *from* the body in such a manner that will allow the physical to exert itself. For, unless there is the arousing, under such conditions, for the *will* of the body to maintain, to gain control, *little* may be accomplished. 486-1

Another way to use imagination relates to a common physical therapeutic recommended by Cayce. This is the "Gold Cure" mentioned earlier. Here, the individual is told to take a mixture of chloride of gold and bromide of soda in order to build up a resistance to drinking. This works by producing an adverse reaction when combined with alcohol, producing nausea and vomiting. The result is the creation of a new habitual response to alcohol. This can be seen in the next excerpt:

> Q. Should any alcoholic stimulant be taken? If so, in what form? Beer, wine or hard liquor?
> A. Naturally, there will be the desire. It should be gradually weakened and weakened; and four or five days—well, he won't want it—without vomiting up his shoe soles! Whether it's hard liquor or what! Alcohol won't work with gold! This is the gold treatment, but it builds the resistance! 606-1

The effectiveness of this, as any treatment, always depended on the determination of the individual. As one person is told:

> Now this will produce such conditions that if strong drink is taken it will nauseate the body. But if there is the disregard of this and the *continued* use of the strong drink, it will make for the noneffectiveness in the system except nausea. 1753-1

In his earlier readings, Cayce recommended other combinations of chemicals that had the same adverse effects when combined with alcohol. As noted above, this approach is a prototype for aversion therapy, a common psychiatric treatment used today in the treatment of alcohol dependence. Here, under the supervision of a physician, a drug called Antabuse (disulfiram) is prescribed. The drug has no effect unless it is combined with alcohol, in which case the individual becomes quite sick. Again, the goal here is to build up a negative reaction to drinking patterns. The use of Antabuse or other drugs is a physical intervention, and it must be employed under the supervision of a physician. However, a variant of aversion therapy, covert sensitization, allows you to work with it on a self-management basis. As we saw earlier, this strategy uses the power of imagination to break bad habits. With alcohol dependence, this involves the creation of a mental movie where drinking is paired with some adverse stimulus. Whether the stimulus is vomiting, sickness, disease, arrest, or whatever, it has to become associated with drinking in your imagination. The trick here is to make the fantasy as real as possible and make use of all your senses. Also needed is the repetition of the fantasy, especially under conditions of relaxation. This is a powerful technique and can prove quite effective.

Another way to work with alcohol dependence is to

use your reason to challenge irrational beliefs and other distortions in thinking. In one reading, Cayce advised a man who was having trouble dealing with his employees' drinking habits to approach them:

> . . . through counsel—not cussing, but through reasoning—that of the desire on the part *of* the individuals, as to the duty first, to the privilege next as the individual has in *serving* in the capacity as they do occupy—this [is] the only way and manner in which these individuals may be reached. 4458-1

A very common irrational belief seen in the alcoholic is the need to rely on something stronger than one's self. This is, of course, the alcohol. The destructive effects of such a belief are obvious. The rational comeback here is to have faith in one's self and in one's abilities. The readings not only agree with this but view this self as emanating from another one, or a Big I. As can be seen here, they tell us that it is the spiritual self that one should rely on:

> For these conditions may be overcome with this body if the entity will turn first to the spiritual self, and seek spiritual aid and guidance from within . . . 1427-1

Another irrational belief often seen in alcohol dependence is the idea that it's easier to avoid problems in life than to face up to them. Whether the problems relate to finances, relationships, school, or other situations in life, the person does not confront them but avoids them through drinking. This belief usually goes hand in hand with the cognitive error seen in blaming. Here, the individual perceives the source of the problem in other people or in life's events. This can be one's boss, spouse, teacher, the stock market, and so on. The list of blame goes on and on. The readings challenge both these ideas by saying that we are responsible for our lives. We have created our present circumstances as a result of recent actions or more remote ones. Moreover, the corrective tendencies of karmic laws constantly put us face to face with ourselves. One individual is told:

> For each soul, each entity, *constantly* meets self. And if each soul would but understand, those hardships which are accredited much to others are caused most by self. *Know* that in those you are meeting *thyself!* 845-4

The cause of the alcohol dependence, then, is in the person, not in outside sources. Furthermore, since responsibility lies here, present drinking patterns can only lead to future consequences which eventually will be encountered. Not only is the individual the source of the problem, but the problem is there for a purpose. In its solution, the person has the opportunity to understand life from its larger perspective. Avoiding the problem through drinking represents another misapplication of will and, as the readings tell us, only makes things worse. Working with imagination and reason can reinforce one's will and foster the development of selflessness in the alcohol dependent individual.

Additional help can come by incorporating behavior into the self-management program. We saw this earlier with the inclusion of bibliotherapy as a stimulus control measure. Another way of working with stimulus control is to place oneself in situations that encourage the expression of more desirable behaviors. Examples of this for the alcohol-dependent person are the elimination of all alcoholic beverages from the home, not frequenting bars, not associating with individuals who drink, and things of this sort. Such situations subdue the temptation to drink. One reading puts it like this:

> Hence we find there are periods or conditions in which the body will swear, declare to self he *will* not—and yet with the associations, the environ that offers the opportunity, these become impelling influences . . . 2161-1

An extreme form of stimulus control is institutionalization. The reading often advised this in more serious cases where will was deteriorated. One individual is advised to go to a sanatorium:

> Then *we* would give that not only must the body-mind turn to the spiritual promises that are a part of its mental and spiritual self, but the environment must be changed; so that the spiritual promises may be put to active service and work to replace the habits with the habits of doing *good,* doing right, doing justice, being merciful. 1427-1

Another way of working more directly with behavior is through the use of aversion techniques. Such techniques incorporate aversion therapy, covert sensitization, and any similar methods, where pleasurable but harmful habits are eliminated by associating them with negative stimuli. In the case of alcohol dependence, this means learning to connect drinking with adverse events. These could include almost anything. Suppose, for example, that you hate housework. In using the aversion technique, you might make a deal with yourself to engage in a certain amount of housework every time you had a drink. The craving would eventually diminish, as it becomes more and more associated with this undesirable activity. Success, of course, depends on your determination and will. Working with behavior also means the expression of physical ideals. Doing good is a recurrent theme of the readings. One individual is told:

> But *find* self not in the gratifying for the moment, not in appetites. Not that anyone is to become goody-goody, but good *for* something! 934-7

The emphasis here is on behavior. The individual is told that being good means applying it or being "good for something." As we have seen, this can be facilitated with the help of positive reinforcement. Behavior that is linked with a reward becomes more easily consolidated as a new habit pattern. A reward can be anything that is pleasing to you, whether it be material, social, or self-generated thoughts. The readings also recommend other psychospiritual techniques that focus on exercise, hobbies, interest, careers, and other strategies. One woman asked Cayce what kind of work or activity would be most beneficial for her alcoholic husband. The reading tells her that:

> There must be some changes from within for the desire to be not only good—at *any* of those problems or those activities that he is well fitted for— but to be good for something for *others* rather than his own appetites. These must be created first. 845-4

Again, the emphasis is on the need for an altruistic foundation, regardless of the chosen activity. In addition to these psychospiritual recommendations, the readings also discuss the need for prayer. Unlike the other psychological disorders, however, they more often encourage the prayers of others, in addition to those of the individual. This was especially advised in those cases where there was a tendency toward possession. Look how poignantly Cayce answers the following question:

> Q. *Can those assisting do anything to prevent the body from indulging in stimulants?*
> A. They can pray like the devil!
> And this is not a blasphemous statement, as it may appear—to some. For if there is any busier body, with those influences that have to do with the spirit of indulgence of any nature, than that ye call satan or the devil, who is it?
> Then it behooves those who have the interest of such a body at heart to not only pray for him but *with* him; and in just as earnest, just as sincere, just as continuous a manner as the spirit of *any* indulgence works upon those who have become subject to such influences either through physical, mental or material conditions!
> For the *power* of prayer is *not* met even by satan or the devil himself. 1439-2

In the other psychological disorders discussed, we saw that meditation is also recommended as a complementary procedure to prayer. This is not the case for alcohol dependence, where it appears to be downplayed. The reason for this is that drinking can sensitize the body to supernatural influences. We saw this regarding its role in possession. As a result, any attempt to meditate may result in serious problems. This may be the reason for the readings' emphasis on prayer in cases of alcohol dependence, both by the individual and by others. A reasonable alternative, then, would be to live one's life as a meditation. Working with ideals in conjunction with prayer can prove quite fruitful here, and as one's resistance to alcohol is strengthened, meditation can be undertaken.

As always, it is important to indicate your target symptom, base rating, goals, and strategy in a written contract before beginning to work on your problem. Remember also the importance of choosing a technique that fits best with your personality style. Finally, be patient in your endeavors and try to apply your efforts in a persistent and consistent manner for the most beneficial results.

14

Changing Your Mind

Keep the eye single to a service for *spiritual* understanding, and a mental aberation or a mental disturbance may not touch thee! Edgar Cayce reading 1442-1

The title of this chapter echoes the theme of the book. To this end, two basic approaches to psychological disorders have been presented. One comes from today's psychology, especially that of the behavioral model. The other represents the viewpoint expressed in the Cayce readings. Each approach stems from very different philosophical backgrounds. This is most evident where the causes of the problem are considered.

The behavioral model looks at a psychological disorder as a maladaptive habit learned during the course of one's life. The acquisition of this habit occurs through respondent conditioning, operant conditioning, or one of its variants, expanded here in the cognitive-behavioral viewpoint. The habit is seen as the immediate cause of the problem and is expressed in psychological and behavioral patterns. In the behavioral model, the human being is considered a complex computer, while the faulty learning is seen as poor "programming." Free will is nonexistent, as all habits reflect an interplay of heredity and environment.

The Cayce perspective, as we have seen, is much more profound. While it also considers the habitual nature of the psychological disorder, it equates habits with patterns that incorporate spiritual dimensions, in addition to mental and physical ones. As a result, psychological problems are evaluated within a context of various remote causes, as well as more immediate factors. Remote causes are linked to the soul. They represent the misapplication of free will by a Big I as it seeks to express itself within the parameters of a divine pattern. This expression has an ideal form which defines the individuality of the soul. Any deviation from this ideal sets into motion karmic corrections which put the Big I back on course. Actions and reactions occur in various spiritual dimensions, each corresponding to different states of consciousness, and each reflecting previous experiences on earth, as well as those occurring between lives. The interaction of patterns represents the habit inherent in the psychological disorder, with its spiritual, mental, physiological, and behavioral components.

The differences between behavioral psychology and the Cayce readings are less pronounced when therapeutics are considered. They both agree that action and application are needed in order to confront the psychological problem and to effect positive changes in one's life. In the behavioral model, such actions are aimed at changing existing habits through reconditioning. Change is equated with alterations in present habit patterns.

Many behavioral techniques have been presented here, as well as some from other psychological models. These techniques have proven to be quite effective in dealing with a variety of psychological disorders.

In the Cayce approach, change is equated with the formation of new habit patterns, rather than the restructuring of old ones. Maladaptive patterns are to be replaced with more adaptive ones. Therapeutics are holistic and address a system of spirit, mind, and body in conflict. Because the habit has a physiological component, therapy is also directed at this level and is more specific as pathology becomes evident. Habit formation, therefore, comprises the development of new patterns of spirit, mind, body, and behavior. Psychospiritual therapeutics also stress the need to recognize the disorder as an opportunity for spiritual growth and actualization. The individual is encouraged to define a spiritual ideal as a guidepost and to apply it in life, both psychologically and behaviorally. The value of systematically incorporating prayer and meditation into such efforts is emphasized.

The various coping strategies from contemporary psychology have been presented as quite compatible to working with ideals. Incorporating these is especially beneficial in today's world of specialization, with its emphasis on self-help through telephones, computers, and "cookbook" manuals, just to name a few. This trend has been accommodated here, regardless of one's goals. The self-management of psychological problems has been presented in a step-by-step fashion, where a written contract with one's self is established in which specific problem areas, goals, and strategies are specified.

We looked at a variety of psychological disorders under the purview of the Cayce readings. These represented the more common complaints present during his lifetime as well as our own. In addition to these, readings were also given for many other psychological problems. These included but were not limited to such conditions as: conversion disorder; hypochondriasis; male erectile disorder; various disorders of childhood and adolescence, like mental retardation, stuttering, oppositional defiant disorder, and enuresis; and schizophrenia, plus other psychotic disorders.

The spectrum of psychological disorders we examined is adequate in providing a sense of the Cayce approach, as all psychological problems have a common source. The focus for any problem revolves around working with ideals. Approaching the problem in this manner not only fosters symptom relief but facilitates the true purpose of life, that of spiritual actualization. As one develops more constructive habit patterns, the recognition comes of the ultimate source of such patterns, the Big I. Along with this, there is the increase in freedom with the realization of one's role as co-creator of such patterns within the framework of a divine pattern. Changing your mind, then, means more than changing present psychological, physiological, and behavioral patterns to alleviate present distress. It means aligning your will within the framework of this divine pattern in order to fulfill your true destiny, that of spiritual becoming. Good luck to you as you work with this opportunity.

Endnotes

Chapter One
Problems, Problems, Problems!

1. The Edgar Cayce readings are indexed by case number. For example, reading 641-6 refers to the sixth reading given to individual #641.

Chapter Two
How Did I Get This Way? The View of Edgar Cayce

1. *There Is a River* is available from A.R.E. Press.

Chapter Three
Are Psychological Disorders Bad Habits?

1. *The Treatment of Depression,* David L. McMillin, pp. 192-195.
2. *Healing Miracles,* William A. McGarey.
3. *The Treatment of Depression,* op. cit.
4. *Keys to Health,* Eric Mein.
5. *The Edgar Cayce Handbook for Health Through Drugless Therapy,* Harold J. Reilly and Ruth Hagy Brod.

Chapter Five
Learning to Relax

1. *Progressive Relaxation,* Edmund Jacobson.
2. *The Relaxation Response,* Herbert Benson.

Chapter Six
Using Your Imagination

1. *Visualization for Change,* Patrick Fanning, pp. 7-23.
2. *The Practice of Behavior Therapy,* Joseph Wolpe.
3. "Tuning In on the Twilight Zone," Thomas Budzynski, *Psychology Today,* August 1977, pp. 38-44.

Chapter Seven
Changing Your Thoughts

1. *The Feeling Good Handbook,* David D. Burns, pp. 8-11.
2. "Rational Psychotherapy," Albert Ellis, in *Psychotherapy and Counseling: Studies in Technique,* William S. Sahakian, ed., pp. 210-225.

CHAPTER NINE
WORKING WITH SPIRITUAL IDEALS
1. *Unto the Churches*, Richard H. Drummond.
2. *Discovering Your Soul's Purpose*, Mark Thurston, pp. 22-25.

CHAPTER TEN
PLANNING YOUR STRATEGY: WHAT ARE YOUR GOALS?
1. *Diagnostic and Statistical Manual of Mental Disorders*, Fourth Edition, American Psychiatric Association.

CHAPTER ELEVEN
ANXIETY DISORDERS: LIVING IN FEAR
1. *Diagnostic and Statistical Manual of Mental Disorders*, Fourth Edition, op. cit., pp. 393-444.
2. Ibid.
3. *Living Nightmares*, David L. McMillin.

CHAPTER TWELVE
DEPRESSION: WHEN SAD FEELINGS WON'T GO AWAY
1. *Diagnostic and Statistical Manual of Mental Disorders*, Fourth Edition, op. cit., pp. 317-391.
2. Ibid.
3. *The Treatment of Depression*, op. cit., pp. 38-88.

CHAPTER THIRTEEN
ALCOHOL DEPENDENCE: DRINKING THAT IS OUT OF CONTROL
1. *Diagnostic and Statistical Manual of Mental Disorders*, Fourth Edition, op. cit., pp. 194-204.

References

1. American Psychiatric Association. *Diagnostic and Statistical Manual of Mental Disorders,* Fourth Edition (Washington, D.C.: American Psychiatric Association, 1994)

2. Benson, Herbert. *The Relaxation Response* (New York: Morrow, 1975)

3. Budzynski, Thomas. "Tuning In on the Twilight Zone." *Psychology Today* (August 1977), 38-44.

4. Burns, David D. *The Feeling Good Handbook* (New York: Penguin Books, 1989)

5. Drummond, Richard H. *Unto the Churches* (Virginia Beach: A.R.E. Press, 1978)

6. Ellis, Albert. "Rational Psychotherapy." *Psychotherapy and Counseling: Studies in Technique,* William S. Sahakian, ed. (Chicago: Rand McNally, 1969)

7. Fanning, Patrick. *Visualization for Change* (Oakland: New Harbinger Publications, 1988)

8. Jacobson, Edmund. *Progressive Relaxation* (Chicago: University of Chicago Press, 1938)

9. McGarey, William A. *Healing Miracles* (Cambridge: Harper & Row, 1988)

10. McMillin, David L. *Living Nightmares* (Virginia Beach: Lifeline Press, 1992)

11. McMillin, David L. *The Treatment of Depression* (Virginia Beach: Lifeline Press, 1991)

12. Mein, Eric. *Keys to Health* (New York: Harper & Row, 1989)

13. Reilly, Harold J. & Brod, Ruth Hagy. *The Edgar Cayce Handbook for Health Through Drugless Therapy* (Virginia Beach: A.R.E. Press, 1975)

14. Sugrue, Thomas. *There Is a River* (New York: Holt, Rinehart & Winston, 1941)

15. Thurston, Mark. *Discovering Your Soul's Purpose* (Virginia Beach: A.R.E. Press, 1984)

16. Wolpe, Joseph. *The Practice of Behavior Therapy* (Elmsford: Pergamon Press, 1969)

A.R.E. Press

The A.R.E. Press publishes quality books, videos, and audiotapes meant to improve the quality of our readers' lives—personally, professionally, and spiritually. We hope our products support your endeavors to realize your career potential, to enhance your relationships, to improve your health, and to encourage you to make the changes necessary to live a loving, joyful, and fulfilling life.

Some titles related to *How to Change Your Mind*, along with their "stock numbers" in case you would like to order any of them directly from us, include:

Discovering Your Soul's Purpose, by Mark Thurston, Ph.D.
A book that will help you discover the path to self-understanding—toward finding what it is you were born to do in this lifetime. Using techniques described in the Edgar Cayce readings and other systems of personal transformation, this book outlines a practical five-step procedure for you to gain insight into your personal mission in life. ISBN 0-87604-157-8, 175 pp. Paperback, **$12.95 #324**

Your Mind: Unlocking Your Hidden Powers, by Henry Reed, Ph.D.
Henry Reed examines Edgar Cayce's revelations about the mind's unlimited creative energy—from the power of visualization to entering altered states, from premonitions to increasing your willpower and understanding your dreams. This book is a guide to discovering the power that resides within us all. ISBN 0-87604-365-1, 258 pp. Paperback, **$14.95 #480**

The Hidden Meaning of Illness: Disease as a Symbol and Metaphor, by Robert Trowbridge, M.Div.
From colds and allergies to life-threatening diseases, our illnesses and symptoms—like the symbols in our dreams—are actually messages from our inner self. Learn how to interpret them and get back on the road to health! ISBN 0-87604-358-9, 279 pp. Paperback, **$13.95 #454**